A Closer Look
at
St. John's Parish
Registers
1701-1801

Henry C. Peden, Jr.

HERITAGE BOOKS
2007

HERITAGE BOOKS

AN IMPRINT OF HERITAGE BOOKS, INC.

Books, CDs, and more—Worldwide

For our listing of thousands of titles see our website
at
www.HeritageBooks.com

Published 2007 by
HERITAGE BOOKS, INC.
Publishing Division
65 East Main Street
Westminster, Maryland 21157-5026

International Standard Book Number: 978-1-58549-843-7

PREFACE

In 1987 I compiled and published *St. John's & St. George's Parish Registers, 1696-1851*. The majority of the vital records pertained to St. John's P. E. Parish in Baltimore County and the remainder was for St. George's P. E. Parish which is now in Harford County. The parish registers and the index had been transcribed by Lucy Harrison many years ago and this was noted in the book. In 1988 Bill and Martha Reamy compiled and published *St. George's Parish Registers, 1689-1793*.

Since the publication of my 1987 book I have discovered many errors that pertained primarily to entries made in the register of St. John's P. E. Parish in the 18th century. I further investigated the records for that time period and compiled this supplemental book which I have titled *A Closer Look at St. John's Parish Registers, 1701-1801*.

Many entries were checked against the original parish records (on microfilm and which were often difficult to read). There were several registers for St. John's that duplicate information. They were apparently recopied by the parish clerk or the minister in subsequent years. This led to errors. The registers are for the years 1696-1788, 1768-1852, 1795-1851, and 1779-1809. They are all available on microfilm at the Maryland State Archives (MSA M416).

In some cases the names and dates in the aforementioned registers were checked against information abstracted and published in Robert W. Barnes' *Maryland Marriages, 1634-1777, Maryland Marriages, 1778-1800*, and *Baltimore County Families, 1659-1759*, Dawn Beitler Smith's *Baltimore County Marriage Licenses, 1777-1798*, and Jon Harlan Livezey and Helene Maynard Davis' *Harford County, Maryland Marriage Licenses, 1777-1865*.

Many errors and omissions that were made by either me or Lucy Harrison, as well as in the above cited books, have been corrected. I have also placed my respective comments in parenthesis after each entry within the text, but some unresolved discrepancies still remain. Be that as it may, I decided to publish these corrections anyway and to share the information with others. Even though it took sixteen years to get around to it, I trust that researchers will find my book to be worth the wait and they will appreciate the effort.

Henry C. Peden, Jr.
Bel Air, Maryland

A CLOSER LOOK AT ST. JOHN'S
PARISH REGISTERS, 1701-1801

Acre, Mary and Hugh Cunningham married in 1749 (the exact date was not given, but apparently they married some time between 26 Mar and 14 May 1749; his name was listed as Cuninghame in the parish register)

Adams, Elizabeth and John Little, both of Harford County, married 20 Jul 1794 (they were married by virtue of the publication of banns)

Adams, Susanna and William Collison married 3 Dec 1713 (their names were listed as William Collason and Susanah Addams in my 1987 book)

Addison, John and Sarah Leitch, both of Baltimore County, married 11 Oct 1792 (they were married by virtue of a license issued on 5 Oct 1792 which listed her name as Sally Leech; his name was listed as John Addison, Jr. in another part of the parish register)

Ady, Jonathan, see "Jonathan Eddee," q.v.

Ady, Joshua (of Harford County) and Mary Ford (of Baltimore County) married 6 Nov 1792 (the parish register indicated they were married by virtue of a license issued in Baltimore County, but no marriage license was found in Baltimore or Harford County)

Airs, Sarah and Jacob Ruth married 2 Sep 1759 (their marriage date was mistakenly entered as 2 Apr 1759 in my 1987 book)

Allen, Ann(e) and John Bruff married 31 Jan 1749 (the date should actually be written 31 Jan 1749/50; another entry in the parish register indicated they married subsequent to 17 Dec 1749, but the exact date was not given)

Allen, Frances, see "Mary Allen," q.v.

Allen, Hannah, see "Robert Thomas Allen," q.v.

Allen, Mary, daughter of Nathaniel and Frances, born 23 Apr 1727 (her name was mistakenly listed as May Alen in my 1987 book)

Allen, Nathaniel, see "Mary Allen," q.v.

Allen, Robert Thomas, son of William and Hannah, born 1 Nov 1801 (his date of birth was mistakenly listed as 1901 in my 1987 book and his mother's name was mistakenly listed as Howard instead of Hannah)

Allen, William, see "Robert Thomas Allen," q.v.

Allender, John Wane, son of William and Sophia, born 5 May 1796 (his name was listed as John Wana Allinder in my 1987 book)

Almeny, John and Elizabeth Waddham married 6 Feb 1753 (another entry in the parish register indicated John Almaney and Eliza Warhorn (probably misspelled) married in 1753, but the exact date was not given)

Amos, Ann and Daniel Cunningham, both of Harford County, married 19 Oct 1797 (they were married by virtue of a license issued on 16 Oct 1797 which listed her name as Amoss; her name was listed as Anna in another part of the parish register)

Amoss, Hannah and Peter Prine married 13 Nov 1760 (his name was listed as Prynne in the parish register and in my 1987 book)

Anderson, Cassandra and Israel Standiford married 6 Jan 1743 (the date should actually be written 6 Jan 1743/4; his name was listed as Standeford in my 1987 book)

Anderson, Cassandra and John Clark, both of Harford County, married 15 Nov 1794 (the parish register indicated they were married by virtue of a license issued in Harford County, but no marriage license was found in Harford or Baltimore County)

Anderson, Elizabeth and John Bennett married 23 Mar 1769 (his name was listed as Benet and her name was listed as Eliz. in the parish register)

Anderson, John and Isabell Carr married 13 Jul 1769 (her name was listed as Isbell in the parish register)

Anderson, Rebeckah and James Durham married 12 Feb 1720 (her first name was misspelled Reneckah in my 1987 book)

Anderson, Thomas and Mary Perdue married 26 Mar 1744 (another entry in the parish register indicated they married 18 Mar 1744)

Anderson, William and Mary Harrard married 21 Aug 1755 (her name was difficult to read in the parish register and it could have been Harrard or Haward)

Andrew, Elizabeth and Robert Saunders married 28 Apr 1765 (her name in the parish register could be either Eliz. Andrew or Andrews)

Andrews, William and Mary Bond married 14 Feb 1732 (his name was mistakenly listed as Andrew in my 1987 book)

Armstrong, Elizabeth and Archibald Standiford married 25 Jun 1754 (his name was listed as Archd. Standeford in the parish register and their marriage was entered among the 1756 marriages)

Armstrong, John, see "Mary Armstrong," q.v.

Armstrong, Kezia, daughter of Solomon and Sarah, born 9 Dec 1745 (her name was misspelled Arsmtrong in my 1987 book)

Armstrong, Mary, daughter of John and Rebecca, born 26 Feb 1735 (her name was misspelled Arsmtrong in my 1987 book)

Armstrong, Rebecca, see "Mary Armstrong," q.v.

Armstrong, Rebecca and John Baton married 1 Sep 1763 (his name was listed as Jno. and her name as Reb. in the parish register)

Armstrong, Sarah, see "Kezia Armstrong," q.v.

Armstrong, Solomon, see "Kezia Armstrong," q.v.

Armstrong, Thomas and Mary Carter married in 1749 (the exact date was not given, but the parish register indicated they married subsequent to 17 Dec 1749; his name was mistakenly listed as Arnstrong in my 1987 book)

Armstrong, Thomas and Sarah Dallerhyde married 28 Dec 1752 (another entry in the parish register indicated they married in 1752, but the exact date was not given, and her name was listed as Dellerhide)

Ash, John and Sabra Milhughs married 8 Feb 1763 (her name was misspelled Sabre in my 1987 book)

Asher, Ann and James Robeson married 7 Jun 1752 (her name was listed as Ashor in my 1987 book)

Asher, Anthony Jr. and Sarah Beven married 19 Dec 1749 (another entry in the parish register indicated Anthony Asher and Sarah Bevan married 26 Nov 1749; the earlier date could have been their intention of marriage or publication of banns)

Asher, Mary and Samuel Wilkinson married 14 Apr 1748 (another entry in the parish register indicated they married 3 Jan 1748; the earlier date could have been their intention of marriage or publication of banns)

Asher, Rachael and Joseph Beven married 15 Jan 1754 (another entry in the parish register indicated Joseph Beaven and Rachel Ashen married circa 1753, but the exact date was not given)

Asher, Sarah and Daniel Nusewonden married 14 Nov 1761 (his name as mistakenly listed as Nuservonden in my 1987 book)

Askew, William (of Baltimore) and Sarah Calwell (of Harford County) married 10 Dec 1795 (the marriage year was mistakenly listed as 1794 in my 1987 book and as 1784 in *Maryland Marriages, 1778-1800*; marriage license was issued in Baltimore County on 9 Dec 1795 and listed her name as Sally)

Asquith, David and Frances Nichols, both of Baltimore County, married 2 Oct 1791 (the parish register indicated they were married by virtue of a license issued in Harford County, but no marriage license was found in Harford or Baltimore County)

Atherton, Richard and Susanah Norriss married 1 Nov 1721 (they were listed in *Maryland Marriages, 1634-1777* as Richard Atherton and Susanna Norris married 1 Nov 1729; however, their marriage was entered in the parish register among the 1721-1722 marriages)

Auger, James and Mary James married 1 Jan 1756 (his name was misspelled Anger in my 1987 book)

Axter, Ann and Peter Foreasay married 4 Nov 1758 (his name was difficult to read in the parish register and it could have been Foreasey or Forcasey)

Back (Bank), Prissella and Thomas Nichols married 10 Feb 1763 (her name was difficult to read in the parish register and it could have been Back, Bank or Banks)

Bailey, Ruth and Richard Gott, both of Baltimore County, married 17 Dec 1795 (they were married by virtue of a license issued on 16 Dec 1795)

Bailey, Sarah and George Collins, both of Baltimore County, married 26 Dec 1790 (although her name was listed as Bayley in the parish register, a marriage license issued 23 Dec 1790 listed her name as Bailey)

Baker, Ann and George Crutchinton married 16 Jun 1768 (her name looked like Ann Bakr. in the parish register)

Baker, Avarilla, see "Sarah Baker" and "Bridget Baker," q.v.

Baker, Bridget, daughter of Charles and Avarilla, born 27 Jul 1727 (her first name was misspelled Birdget in my 1987 book)

Baker, Bridget and Edward Brusbanks married 23 Jun 1743 (another entry in the parish register indicated Edward Brusbanks, Jr. and Briggett Baker married 19 Jun 1743)

Baker, Charles, son of Indimeon and Sarah, born -- Aug 1746 (his father's name was mistakenly listed as Indemuel in my 1987 book)

Baker, Charles, see "Sarah Baker" and "Bridget Baker," q.v.

Baker, Cordelia and Morgan Jones, both of Harford County, married 25 Jan 1798 (the parish register indicated they were married by virtue of a license issued on 24 Jan 1798; *Harford County Marriage Licenses, 1777-1865* indicated the license was issued on 25 Jan 1798 and her first name was not listed)

Baker, Hannah and Stephen White married 1 Jan 1751 (another entry in the parish register indicated they married in 1751, but the exact date was not given)

Baker, Indimeon, see "Charles Baker," q.v.

Baker, James and Catherine Smith married 25 Sep 1742 (her name was misspelled Cathrene in my 1987 book)

Baker, Mary and Joseph Frost married 2 Oct 1761 (his name was listed as Jos. or Jas. in my 1987 book)

Baker, Sarah, daughter of Charles and Avarilla, born 23 Aug 1718 (although her date of birth was listed as 23 Aug 17-- in my 1987 book, it was noted as 23 Aug 1718 in *Baltimore County Families, 1659-1759*)

Baker, Sarah, see "Charles Baker," q.v.

Balch, Hezekiah James and Martha McKinley married 27 -- 1768 (probably married 27 Oct 1768, but the information was incomplete in the parish register; his first name was mistakenly misspelled Hankeah in my 1987 book)

Bank, Prissella, see "Prissella Back," q.v.

Barham, Joseph, see "Joseph Boram," q.v.

Barkabee, Ann and William Watkins married 9 Dec 1741 (this marriage was entered in the parish register among the 1752 marriages; see the Anne Blackaby entry herein; the women's names sound quite similar and both men are named William Watkins)

Barns, Robert and Morra Brian married 21 Jul 1766 (his last name was difficult to read in the parish register, but it could be Barns or Borns)

Barton, Ann, daughter of Asael and Susanna, born 15 Dec 1794 (this entry was inadvertently omitted from my 1987 book)

Barton, Ann and Aquila Galloway, both of Baltimore County, married 4 Mar 1792 (their marriage date was mistakenly listed as 4 Apr 1792 in my 1987 book; they were married by virtue of a license issued on 18 Feb 1792 which listed their names as Acquila Galloway and Nancy Barton)

Barton, Ann and Robert Evans married 22 Aug 1771 (their names were listed as Robert Evins and Ann Bartinn in the parish register)

Barton, Asael and Susanna Millikin, both of Baltimore County, married 27 Dec 1791 ("codem die ambo 27th Dec." was written above their names in the parish register; they were married by virtue of a license issued on 20 Dec 1791 which listed her name as Susannah Milliken)

Barton, Asael, see "Margarett Wooden Barton" and "Ann Barton," q.v.

Barton, Elizabeth and John Green married 25 Aug 1763 (his name was mistakenly listed as John Breen in my 1987 book)

Barton, Katheran Happuck and Benn Biddle married 22 Feb 1770 (her name seemed unusual and perhaps it could have been a misspelling of Karenhappuck which was a more common name at that time; Benn was apparently a nickname for Benjamin)

Barton, Margarett Wooden, daughter of Asael and Susanna, born 4 Mar 1793, baptized 14 Jul 1793 (her date of baptism was omitted from my 1987 book)

Barton, Mary, see "Mary Baxton," q.v.

Barton, Mary and Anthony Lynch, both of Baltimore County, married 21 Jun 1792 (they were married by virtue of a license issued on 15 Jun 1792; his name was listed as Antony in another part of the parish register)

Barton, Sim., see "Vissey Price," q.v.

Barton, Susanna, see "Ann Barton" and "Margarett Wooden Barton," q.v.

Bashet, Richard, see "Richard Baskett," q.v.

Baskett, Richard and Adfire Boyd married 31 Jan 1743 (the date should actually be written 31 Jan 1743/4; another entry in the parish register indicated Richard Basket and Adfia Boyd married subsequent to 29 Jan 1744; *Maryland Marriages, 1634-1777* indicated Richard Bashet and Afria Boyd married 29 Jan 1744 and also indicated Richard Basket and Adfire Boyd married 31 Jan 1743)

Baton, John and Rebecca Armstrong married 1 Sep 1763 (his name was listed as Jno. and her name as Reb. in the parish register)

Baxter, Sarah and Thomas Stocksdale, both of Harford County, married 18 Dec 1797 (they were married by virtue of a license issued on that same day)

Baxton (Barton), Mary and William Cantwell married 23 May 1768 (the parish register is unclear; her name could be Baxton or Barton)

Bayley, Cathrine and Thomas Hatten married 29 Jan 1767 (his name was misspelled Hatlin in my 1987 book)

Bayley, Groombright and Mary Moore married 5 Oct 1757 (his name was listed as Groome Bright Bayley in the parish register and in my 1987 book)

Bayley, Keziah and Chainey Hatten married 31 Dec 1761 (her name was listed as Kez. in the parish register)

Bayley, Mary and Mosess Greer married "in the month of January, 1737" (this marriage was entered in the parish register among the 1753 marriages)

Bayley, Thomas Jr. and Rachel Towson married 26 Dec 1758 (his name was mistakenly listed as Thomas Bayley Bayley, Jr. in the parish register and in my 1987 book)

Beard, Cassandra and Edward Edwards married 1 Apr 1762 (her name was listed as Cas. in the parish register)

Beaver, Mary and John Morris (son of Edward) married 25 Feb 1768 (his name was listed as "Jno. Morris, son Edward" in the parish register)

Beaver, Sarah and Timothy News married 13 Dec 1764 (his name was listed as New in my 1987 book)

Bechley (Bochley), Cathrine, see "Cathrine Brokley," q.v.

Bechley (Bochley), Frances and Josias Middlemore married 9 Oct 1720 (their names were listed as Josias Midlemore and Frances Bochley in my 1987 book)

Beck, Clement and William Tucker married 9 Feb 1762 (her name was entered as Clement Beck in the parish register, but this was probably Clemency Beck, born 1742, daughter of Matthew Beck)

Beck, Matthew, see "Clement Beck," q.v.

Beck, Samuel and Mary Groves married 5 Dec 1753 (another entry in the parish register indicated they married in 1753, but the exact date was not given)

Bellows, Ann and William Hughes married 24 Jun 1743 (his name was listed as Hughs in my 1987 book)

Benbow, Juliana and William Wright married 5 Sep 1714 (their names were listed as William Right and Juliana Benbo in my 1987 book)

Benkin (Burkin), John and Mary Fell married 9 Feb 1765 (his name in the parish register could be either Jno. Benkin, Binkin or Burkin)

Bennett, Charles and Martha Collins married 11 Sep 1753 (another entry in the parish register indicated they married in 1753, but the exact date was not given and his name was listed as Bennet)

Bennett, John and Elizabeth Anderson married 23 Mar 1769 (his name was listed as Benet and her name was listed as Eliz. in the parish register)

Bennett, William and Mary Parker married 6 Feb 1753 (another entry in the parish register indicated they married in 1753, but the exact date was not given)

Benson, Thomas and Isabella Brown married 23 Jan 1753 (another entry in the parish register indicated they married in 1752, but the exact date was not given, and her name was listed as Esabellah)

Bertram, Margrett, see "Margaret Butram," q.v.

Beven, John and Anne Turner married 6 Sep 1743 (another entry indicated they married 17 Jul 1743 and his name was listed as Bevan; the earlier date could have been their intention of marriage or publication of banns)

Beven, Joseph and Rachael Asher married 15 Jan 1754 (another entry in the parish register indicated Joseph Beaven and Rachel Ashen married circa 1753, but the exact date was not given)

Beven, Sarah and Anthony Asher, Jr. married 19 Dec 1749 (another entry in the parish register indicated Anthony Asher and Sarah Bevan married 26 Nov 1749; the earlier date could have been their intention of marriage or publication of banns)

Bevins, John Jr. and Sarah ---- married -- Dec 1723 (information was incomplete in the parish register; this marriage was inadvertently omitted from *Maryland Marriages, 1634-1777*)

Bickerton (Bixerton), John and Ann Peaifers or Peaiters married circa 1765 (the exact date of marriage was not given, but their request to publish marriage banns was entered in the parish register some time between 28 Apr 1765 and 20 Jul 1766; John's name was listed as Bickerton and Bixerton in the parish register; Ann had an unusual last name which may have been either Peaifers or Peaiters)

Biddeston, Sosia and Daniel Watkins married 3 May 1770 (his name was listed as Danial in my 1987 book and she was actually Presioca Biddison, daughter of Thomas Biddison)

Biddison, Ann, daughter of Meshack and Kerrenhappuck, born 11 Mar 1798 (this entry was inadvertently omitted from my 1987 book)

Biddison, Kerenhappuck, see "Ann Biddison" and "Salem Biddison" and "Shadrack Biddison," q.v.

Biddison, Mesheck, see "Ann Biddison" and "Salem Biddison" and "Shadrack Biddison," q.v.

Biddison, Presioca, see "Sosia Biddeston," q.v.

Biddison, Salem, son of Mesheck and Kerenhappuck, born 31 Mar 1791 (the date was listed as 30 Mar 1791 in my 1987 book, but it looked like it could have been 31 Mar and his first name could have been listed as Salam)

Biddison, Shadrack, son of Meshack and Kerenhappuck, born 17 Nov 1795 (this information was mistakenly listed in my 1987 book as Shadrick Biddison, son of Mesheck and Kanenhappuck Biddison, born 11 Mar 1795)

Biddison, Thomas, see "Sosia Biddeston," q.v.

Biddle, Benn and Katheran Happuck Barton married 22 Feb 1770 (her name seemed unusual and perhaps it could have been a misspelling of Karenhappuck which was a more common name at that time; Benn was apparently a nickname for Benjamin)

Billingsley, Basil and Ruth Smithson married 29 Jan 1767 (his name was listed as Bazl. in the parish register)

Billingsley, James and Ruth Gilbert married 16 Jun 1767 (his name was misspelled as Billinsgley in my 1987 book)

Billingsley, Walter and Ruth Clarke married 13 Feb 1772 (his name was listed as Billinsley in the parish register)

Birkhead, Thomas and Elizabeth Waters, both of Baltimore County, married 7 Dec 1797 (they were married by virtue of a license issued on 4 Dec 1797; *Baltimore County Marriage Licenses, 1777-1798* mistakenly listed his name as Bukhead)

Bishop, Mary and Joseph Lair married 7 Jan 1742 (the date should actually be written 7 Jan 1742/3; another entry in the parish register indicated they married 19 Dec 1742 and his name was listed as Lare; the earlier date could have been their intention of marriage or publication of banns)

Blackaby, Anne and William Watkins married in summer of 1742 "on W. Carbel's land" (see the Ann Barkabee entry herein; the women's names sound quite similar and both men are named William Watkins)

Blackett (Bracket), Ann and William Leggett married 13 Jul 1750 (another entry in the parish register indicated William Legat and Martha Bracket married some time between February and August, 1750, but the exact date was not given)

Blunden, James and Sarah Eights married 1 Dec 1759 (his name was mistakenly listed as Blunder in my 1987 book)

Boarding, Martha and Arnold Holt married 11 Feb 1744 (another entry in the parish register indicated they married 10 Feb 1745; the date should actually be written 11 Feb 1744/5)

Bochley, Frances, see "Frances Bechley," q.v.

Bond, Buckler and Charity Bond married 17 Apr 1770 (his name was misspelled as Buckley in the parish register)

Bond, Cassandra and James Scott married 15 Apr 1770 (her name was listed as Casandera in the parish register)

Bond, Charity, see "Buckler Bond," q.v.

Bond, Mary and William Andrews married 14 Feb 1732 (his name was mistakenly listed as Andrew in my 1987 book)

Bond, Peggy and John Hambleton, both of Harford County, married 17 Jun 1793 (they were married by virtue of a license issued that same day and listed her name as Margaretta Bond)

Bond, Penelopy and John Hows married 22 Jul 1750 (another entry in the parish register indicated John House and Penelope Bond married some time between February and August, 1750, but the exact date was not given)

Bond, Sally Charity and Moses Maxwell, both of Harford County, married 10 Dec 1793 (the parish register indicated they were married by virtue of a license issued in Harford County, but no marriage license was found in Harford or Baltimore County)

Bond, Thomas and Rebeckah Stansbury married 19 Dec 1771 (her name was mistakenly listed as Reneckah in my 1987 book)

Bonney, Alce and Hezekiah Day married 12 Jul 1713 (her maiden name was mistakenly listed as Alce Bonney Day in my 1987 book)

Boone, Elizabeth and Robert Howlet married in 1771 (the exact date of marriage was not given, but their request to publish marriage banns was entered in the parish register some time between 27 Jul 1771 and 15 Sep 1771)

Boram, Joseph and Sarah Demmet married 7 Aug 1753 (another entry in the parish register indicated Joseph Barham and Sarah Demmett married in 1753, but the exact date was not given)

Borns, Robert, see "Robert Barns," q.v.

Bosley, Caleb and Elizabeth Wheeler married 27 Feb 1772 (his name was listed as Calib Bozley in the parish register)

Bosley, Cueler and John Helm married 2 Sep 1762 (her name was listed as Bozley in the parish register)

Bosley, Diana and Elias Majors married 8 Sep 1763 (her name was listed as Bozley in my 1987 book)

Bosley, Elisha and Elizabeth Merryman married 29 Jun 1769 (his name was listed as Bozley in my 1987 book)

Bosley, Elizabeth, see "Jeselila Bosley," q.v.

Bosley, Elizabeth and Vincent Talbott married 2 Feb 1773 (her name was listed as Bozley in my 1987 book)

Bosley, Elizabeth and William Hadmington married 23 Mar 1769 (her name was listed as Bozley in my 1987 book)

Bosley, Ezekiel and Elizabeth Norris married 21 Oct 1760 (his name was listed as Ezikiel Bozley in the parish register)

Bosley, James and Rachel Gorsuch married 18 Sep 1760 (their names were listed as James Bozley and Rachl. Gorsuch in the parish register)

Bosley, Jeselila, daughter of William and Elizabeth, born 10 Jun 1745 (her name was listed as Jesclila Bozley in my 1987 book)

Bosley, Martha and Vincent Trapnell married 20 Nov 1768 (her name was mistakenly listed as Marth Bozley in my 1987 book)

Bosley, Prudence and Daniel Shaw married 14 Apr 1763 (her name was listed as Bozley in the parish register)

Bosley, Vincent and Wheelamina Norris married 28 Mar 1771 (his name was listed as Bozley in my 1987 book)

Bosley, William, see "Jeselila Bosley," q.v.

Boswell, Ann(e) and David Shadows married 26 Dec 1749 (another entry in the parish register indicated they married subsequent to 17 Dec 1749, but the exact date was not given, and her name was listed as Anne Bozwell)

Boswell, John and Mary Jennings married 17 Nov 1745 (another entry in the parish register listed their names as Bozwell and Jenings)

Boswell, Thomas and Mary Chanley or Chamney married -- May 1752 (the exact date was not given; another entry indicated Thomas Buswell and Mary Chamney married 30 Aug 1752; the earlier date could have been their intention of marriage or publication of banns)

Botts, Sarah and Richard Butler, both of Harford County, married 29 Dec 1792 (this marriage was inadvertently omitted from my 1987 book; they were married by virtue of a license issued on 27 Dec 1792)

Boulson, John, see "John Poulson," q.v.

Bowen, Mary, see "Mary Bown," q.v.

Bowen, William and Elizabeth Moss married 16 Sep 1753 (another entry in the parish register indicated they married in 1753, but the exact date was not given and his name was listed as Bowing)

Bowers, John and Hannah Bronwell or Bromwell, both of Harford County, married 3 Jul 1793 (her name was listed as Bronnell in my 1987 book and in *Maryland Marriages, 1778-1800*, as Bronwell in another part of the parish register, and as Bromwell on the marriage license issued on 3 Jul 1793)

Bowles, Peter and Rachel Coen, both of Harford County, married 17 Jul 1788 (her name was mistakenly listed as Coon in my 1987 book)

Bown, Mary and Joseph Green married 25 Feb 1744 (the date should actually be written 25 Feb 1744/5; another entry in the parish register indicated Joseph Green and Mary Bowen married 24 Feb 1745)

Boyce, John and Elizabeth Jephs married 30 Nov 1721 (his name was listed as Boice in my 1987 book and her name, although unusual, was listed as shown here)

Boyd, Adfire and Richard Baskett married 31 Jan 1743 (the date should actually be written 31 Jan 1743/4; another entry in the parish register indicated Richard Basket and Adfia Boyd married subsequent to 29 Jan 1744; *Maryland Marriages, 1634-1777* indicated Richard Bashet and Afria Boyd married 29 Jan 1744 and also indicated Richard Basket and Adfire Boyd married 31 Jan 1743)

Boyd, Elizabeth and Andrew Jenkins married 12 Jan 1743 (the date should actually be written 12 Jan 1743/4; another entry in the parish register indicated Henry Jenkins and Elizabeth Boyd married 25 Dec 1743; the earlier date could have been their intention of marriage or publication of banns)

Bozman, Edward and Rozannah Lyon married 27 Feb 1749 (the date should actually be written 27 Feb 1749/50; another entry in the parish register indicated Edward Bosman and Rose Lyon married some time after 11 Feb 1750, but the exact date was not given)

Bradfield, Elizabeth and Robert Robell married 23 Mar 1746 (the date should actually be written 23 Mar 1746/7; another entry in the parish register indicated Robert Cabell and Elizabeth Bradfield married 3 Nov 1746; the earlier date could have been their intention of marriage or publication of banns)

Bradford, Elizabeth, see "Joseph Bradford," q.v.

Bradford, Joseph, son of William and Elizabeth, born 15 Jan 1718 (although his date of birth was listed as 15 Jan 17-- in my 1987 book, it was noted as 15 Jan 1718 in *Baltimore County Families, 1659-1759*)

Bradford, Sarah and James Fullerton, both of Harford County, married 13 Jan 1791 (the parish register indicated they were married by virtue of a license from Harford County, but no marriage license was found in Harford or Baltimore County)

Bradford, William and Sarah McComas married 16 Feb 1764 (her name was listed as M'Comus in the parish register)

Bradford, William, see "Joseph Bradford," q.v.

Bradley, John and Anne Evans married 2 Oct 1743 (another entry in the parish register indicated they married 4 Sep 1743 and listed her name as Evens; the earlier date could have been their intention of marriage or publication of banns; the 2 Oct 1743 marriage was entered on page 127 of the register and the 4 Sep 1743 marriage was entered on page 239, but both references to Bradley were missing from the index to my 1987 book)

Brannan, Frances and John Woaler (Waaler) married 4 Apr 1768 (his name was listed as Woaler in my 1987 book and as Wooler in *Maryland Marriages, 1634-1777*, but it looked liked Waaler in the parish register)

Brannian, John and Sarah George, both of Harford County, married 23 Jun 1791 (his name was listed as Branian in my 1987 book and Brannion in the parish register; his name was listed as Brannian when issued a marriage license on 21 Jun 1791)

Braser, Sarah and ---- Darymple married in summer of 1742 "in the forest" (*Maryland Marriages, 1634-1777* listed it as "(?) Darumple married Sarah Braser, no date given")

Breavinton (Brewenton), Winiford and Robert Cutchin married 20 Apr 1731 (her name was listed as Brewenton in my 1987 book and as Breavinton in *Baltimore County Families, 1659-1759*)

Bremer, Barbara and William Ellenor (Ellender), both of Baltimore County, married 19 Feb 1795 (although his last name was listed as Ellenor in the parish register, it could have been Ellender; her name was mistakenly listed as Bemer in my 1987 book and as Bemer or Berner in *Maryland Marriages,*

1778-1800; however, no license was found in Baltimore or Harford County
in order to verify the spelling of the name)

Brian, James and Mary Raven married 4 Jul 1754 (her name was listed as
Reaven in the parish register)

Brian, Morra and Robert Barns married 21 Jul 1766 (his last name was difficult
to read in the parish register, but it could be Barns or Borns)

Brian, William and Hannah Wallis married 5 May 1746 (another entry in the
parish register indicated William Bryan and Hannah Wallace married 13 Apr
1746; the earlier date could have been their intention of marriage or
publication of banns)

Brierly, Margarett and William Cunningham married ---- (no date was given,
but the marriage appeared between entries made on 29 Dec and 31 Dec 1761
in the parish register; his name was listed as Wm. Cuninggam)

Bringingham, Margery and Edward Fairchild married 6 Dec 1761 (her name
was listed as Margarey in my 1987 book)

Britain, Cathrine and Thomas Clark married 21 Nov 1749 (another entry in the
parish register indicated Thomas Clerk and Kathrine Breton married between
24 Sep and 26 Nov 1749, but the exact date was not given)

Broad, Barbara and James Demmitt married 27 Mar 1723 (his name was listed
as Demmett and her first name was misspelled as Barbaro in my 1987 book)

Broad, Jane and William Edwards married 17 Sep 1748 (another entry in the
parish register indicated they married subsequent to 4 Sep 1748, but the
exact date was not given)

Brokley (Bochley?), Cathrine and William Jones married 23 Dec 1744 (another
entry in the parish register indicated they married on this date, but listed her
name as Katharine Bochley or Bechley)

Bromwell (Bronwell), Hannah and John Bowers, both of Harford County,
married 3 Jul 1793 (her name was listed as Bronnell in my 1987 book and in
Maryland Marriages, 1778-1800, as Bronwell in another part of the parish
register, and as Bromwell on the marriage license issued on 3 Jul 1793)

Brooke (Brookes), Pennil and Simon Hutchenson married 12 Aug 1750 (another
entry in the parish register indicated Simon Hutchison and Penelope Brooke
married in August 1750, but the day was not given)

Brooks, Anne and Philip Cordsman married in 1753 (the complete date was not
given in the parish register)

Brooks, James and Mary Kinnerly married 13 Feb 1774 (her name was listed as
Kinnedy in my 1987 book)

Brooks, Joseph and Elizabeth Phillips married 28 May 1747 (another entry in
the parish register indicated they married 1 Jun 1747)

Brown, Ann and John Wharton married 28 Jan 1744 (another entry in the parish
register indicated they married 28 Jan 1745 and her name was listed as
Anne; the date should actually be written 28 Jan 1744/5)

Brown, Ann and Moses Long married 13 Sep 1764 (his name was listed as Mos.
Long in the parish register)

Brown, Comfort and John Rowing married 14 Feb 1751 (another entry in the parish register indicated they married in 1751, but the exact date was not given, and his name was listed as Rownes)

Brown, Isaac and Elinor Campbell married 13 Jul 1713 (their names were listed as Isack Brown and Elimor Campell in my 1987 book)

Brown, Isabella and Thomas Benson married 23 Jan 1753 (another entry in the parish register indicated they married in 1752, but the exact date was not given, and her name was listed as Esabellah)

Brown, James and Rebecca Wood married 31 May 1767 (her name was listed as Reba. with an elevated "a" in the parish register)

Brown, John and Comfort White married 21 Feb 1747 (the date should actually be written 21 Feb 1747/8; another entry in the parish register indicated they married subsequent to 31 Jan 1748, but the exact date was not given)

Brown, Sarah and John Mullen married 16 Jan 1743 (the date should actually be written 16 Jan 1743/4; another entry in the parish register indicated John Moulins and Sarah Brown married 15 Jan 1743)

Brown, Thomas and Kezia Fraisher married 13 Apr 1760 (her name was listed as Kezia Phraisher in the parish register and in my 1987 book)

Brown, Thomas and Hannah Murray, both of Baltimore County, married 29 Jul 1793 (they were married by virtue of the publication of banns; her name was listed as Murrey in my 1987 book)

Bruceton, Judea and Benjamin Legoe Jr. married 25 Oct 1740 (her name was listed as Judea Briceton or Buceton in my 1987 book and as Judeax Bruceton in *Maryland Marriages, 1634-1777*)

Bruff, John and Ann(e) Allen married 31 Jan 1749 (the date should actually be written 31 Jan 1749/50; another entry in the parish register indicated they married subsequent to 17 Dec 1749, but the exact date was not given)

Brusbanks, Edward and Bridget Baker married 23 Jun 1743 (another entry in the parish register indicated Edward Brusbanks, Jr. and Briggett Baker married 19 Jun 1743)

Bryan, John, see "John O'Bryan," q.v.

Bryan, William, see "William Brian," q.v.

Buceton, Judea, see "Judea Bruceton," q.v.

Buck, Benjamin, son of Christopher and Kezia, born 13 Dec 1795 (the date was listed as 18 Dec 1795 in my 1987 book and the name Kezia was misspelled as Heziah)

Buck, Benjamin Merryman, son of John and Catherine, born 18 Jun 1797 (his middle name was misspelled Merriman in my 1987 book)

Buck, Catherine and John, see "Benjamin Merryman Buck," q.v.

Buck, Christopher and Kezia, see "Benjamin Buck," q.v.

Buck, Joshua, see "Sarah Buck," q.v.

Buck, Sarah, daughter of Joshua and Sarah, born 3 Mar 1798 (this entry was inadvertently omitted from my 1987 book)

Budd, Sarah and Daniel Moores, both of Harford County, married 1 Jan 1793 (they were married by virtue of a license issued on 3 Dec 1792 and listed her name as Sally)

Bull, Cathrene Warden and William Demmitt, Jr. married 6 Oct 1736 (his name was listed without the Jr. in my 1987 book)

Burgess, Susanna and John Conner married -- Aug 1744 (her name was listed as Susannah Burges in my 1987 book)

Burgis (Burgess), Richard and Sarah Castle married -- Oct 1749 (another entry in the parish register indicated Richard Burgess and Sarah Caswell married 20 Aug 1749; the earlier date could have been their intention of marriage or publication of banns)

Burk, Elizabeth and Joshua Legatt married 6 May 1766 (his name was listed as Jos. Legatt in one part of the parish register, yet there was a subsequent entry among the 1771 requests for publication of marriage banns that listed Joshua Legett and Elizabeth Burk, but the exact date was not given)

Burk, Sarah and Thos. Miller married 24 Jul 1748 (another entry in the parish register indicated they married in July 1748, but the exact date was not given; his name was listed as Theophilus instead of Thomas in my 1987 book)

Burk, Ulick and Mary Leekings married 14 May 1732 (his name was mistakenly listed as Buck in my 1987 book)

Burke, Thomas, see "U. Burke," q.v.

Burke, U. and Mary Lemmon married 8 Nov 1764 (his name was mistakenly listed as W. Burke in my 1987 book and he was probably Ulick Burke, born 1740, son of Thomas Burke and grandson of Ulick Burke)

Burkin, John, see "John Benkin," q.v.

Burnet, John and Hannah Spencer, both of Harford County, married 28 Nov 1788 (his name was listed as Burnett and their marriage date was mistakenly listed as 23 Nov 1788 in my 1987 book)

Burns, ---- and Thomas Knight married 18 Jul 1763 (her first name was not indicated in the parish register)

Burns, Isaac and ---- Duwaull married 31 Mar 1761 (her first name was not indicated in the parish register)

Burrough, Sarah and John Ward married 17 Dec 1737 (her name was listed as Borrough in my 1987 book)

Burton, Joseph and Constant Legatt married 13 -- 1768 (probably married 13 Oct 1768, but the information was incomplete in the parish register)

Burton, Ruth and Ralph Yarley, both of Baltimore County, married 24 Dec 1795 (her name was mistakenly listed as Barton in my 1987 book; they were married by virtue of a license issued on 19 Dec 1795 which listed his name as Yarly)

Bush, Mary and John Cope married 5 Feb 1748 (this marriage was entered in the parish register among the 1747 marriages and another entry in the parish register indicated they married subsequent to 31 Jan 1748, but the exact date was not given)

Buswell, Thomas, see "Thomas Boswell," q.v.

Butler, Daniel and Mary Whitaker married 4 Oct 1747 (another entry in the parish register indicated they married 23 Aug 1747; the earlier date could have been their intention of marriage or publication of banns)

Butler, Richard and Sarah Botts, both of Harford County, married 29 Dec 1792 (this marriage was inadvertently omitted from my 1987 book; they were married by virtue of a license issued on 27 Dec 1792)

Butram, Margaret and James Freeman married 28 Oct 1742 (another entry in the parish register listed her name was Margrett Bertram and their marriage date as 10 Oct 1742; the earlier date could have been their intention of marriage or publication of banns)

Byfoot, Moses and Sarah Tayman married 5 Sep 1749 (her name was listed as Tayman or Layman in my 1987 book; another entry in the parish register indicated they married 27 Aug 1749; the earlier date could have been their intention of marriage or publication of banns)

Cabell, Robert, see "Robert Robell," q.v.

Cadle, Ann and James Dorney married 9 Aug 1749 (another entry in the parish register indicated they married some time in May 1749 and spelled her name Caddle; the earlier date could have been their intention of marriage or publication of banns)

Cain, James and Elizabeth Doyle married 30 Dec 1744 (another entry in the parish register indicated they married 25 Dec 1744)

Calwell, Sarah (of Harford County) and William Askew (of Baltimore) married 10 Dec 1795 (the marriage year was mistakenly listed as 1794 in my 1987 book and as 1784 in *Maryland Marriages, 1778-1800*; marriage license was issued in Baltimore County on 9 Dec 1795 and listed her name as Sally)

Cameron, Absolom, son of John and Sarah, born -- Sep 1737 (their names were misspelled as Absolem Comoran and John Camoran in my 1987 book)

Cameron, John and Margaret Macckelltons married 12 Dec 1716 (their names were listed as John Cammeron and Margret Macckelltons in the parish register and in my 1987 book)

Cameron, John and Sarah, see "Absolom Cameron," q.v.

Cammall, John and Margret Meds or Meeds married 17 Mar 1769 (her last name was listed incorrectly as Msds. in my 1987 book)

Campbell, Elinor and Isaac Brown married 13 Jul 1713 (their names were listed as Isack Brown and Elimor Campell in my 1987 book)

Campbell, John and Ann(e) Stevens married 7 Apr 1751 (the exact date was not given in my 1987 book; his name was listed as Cammell in the parish register)

Campbell, Mosess and Rebecca Hughson married "in the month of June, 1751" (this marriage was entered in the parish register among the 1758 marriages)

Cane, Elizabeth, see "Elizabeth Keen," q.v.

Cantwell, Blanch and John Gray married 30 Sep 1750 (her name was misspelled Blansh in my 1987 book)

Cantwell, Mary and John Handland married in 1749 (the exact date was not given, but it was apparently some time in July 1749)

Cantwell, William and Mary Baxton married 23 May 1768 (the parish register is unclear, but her name could be Baxton or Barton)

Carback, Ann and Joseph Wells married 30 Jan 1748 (the date should actually be written 30 Jan 1748/9; another entry in the parish register indicated they

married some time between December, 1748 and February, 1749, but the
exact date was not given; the earlier date could have been their intention of
marriage or publication of banns)

Carback, Ruth and Abraham Green married 25 Jun 1770 (her name was listed as
Ruthe Curbeck in my 1987 book and another entry in the parish register
listed her name as Ruth Carback)

Carback, Valentine and Rachael Colls married 14 Sep 1769 (his name was
mistakenly listed as Corback in my 1987 book)

Cardel, James and Elizabeth Greaves married 17 Feb 1760 (this marriage was
mistakenly listed as February 71, 1760 in my 1987 book)

Carey, Henry and Elizabeth Waller married -- Jul 1746 (another entry in the
parish register indicated Henry Kersey and Elizabeth Whealand married 21
Jul 1746; his name may have been Casey or Kersey although he was listed as
Carey in my 1987 book; *Maryland Marriages, 1634-1777* has the marriage
listed as "Henry Carey and Eliza Waller, 1746")

Carlile, Elizabeth and William Standiford married 16 Jul 1750 (her name was
listed as Eliz. in the parish register and his name was listed as Standeford in
my 1987 book)

Carlisle, Eleanor (Mrs.) and Joseph Presbury married 11 Jul 1723 (their names
were listed as Joseph Presbury and Mrs. Elinor Ca---- in my 1987 book and
as Joseph Presbury and Eleanor Carlisle in *Maryland Marriages, 1634-1777*)

Carr, Isabell and John Anderson married 13 Jul 1769 (her name was listed as
Isbell in the parish register)

Carr, Margarett and Peter Long, both of Harford County, married 30 Aug 1791
(the parish register indicated they were married by virtue of a license from
Harford County, but no marriage license was found in Harford or Baltimore
County)

Carroll, Benjamin and Milly Proctor or Preston, both of Harford County,
married 25 Dec 1792 (his name was listed as Carrol in the parish register and
although her name appeared to be Milly Preston it was listed as Mills Proctor
in my 1987 book and in *Maryland Marriages, 1778-1800*; however, no
marriage license was found in Baltimore or Harford County to verify the
spelling because they were married by virtue of the publication of banns)

Carroll, Delia and Nathan Horner, both of Harford County, married 2 May 1799
(another entry in the parish register mistakenly listed his name as Former;
they were married by virtue of a license issued on 30 Apr 1799 and listed his
name as Horner)

Carroll, Eleanor and James Price married 15 Apr 1770 (her name was listed as
Elinor Carrol in the parish register)

Carroll, John and Cassandra Welch married 24 Dec 1760 (his name was listed as
Jno. and her name was listed as Cas. in the parish register)

Carroll, Peter and Anne Hitchcock married 8 Jun 1739 (his name was listed as
Carrall in my 1987 book)

Carroll, Peter and Martha Clarke married 7 Oct 1770 (his name was listed as
Carrol in the parish register)

Carrothers, George and Jane Mitchell married 18 Feb 1768 (their names in the parish register appeared to be Geo. Carrothus and Jane Mitchl. and this was so noted in *Maryland Marriages, 1634-1777*)

Carson, Jane and William Prigg married 27 Jan 1745 (the date should actually be written 27 Jan 1745/6; another entry in the parish register indicated they married 26 Jan 1746 and listed her name as Jean Carsan)

Cartee, Brian and Frances Leshordie married 2 Jan 1750 (this marriage was entered in the parish register among the January, 1751 marriages; the date should actually be written 2 Jan 1750/1)

Carter, Mary and Thomas Armstrong married in 1749 (the exact date was not given, but the parish register indicated they married subsequent to 17 Dec 1749; his name was mistakenly listed as Arnstrong in my 1987 book)

Cartwright, Mary and Henry Hart married 12 Dec 1780 (her name was mistakenly listed as Mart in my 1987 book)

Carty, Francis and Magdalen Juel, both of Harford County, married 1 Oct 1792 (they were married by virtue of the publication of banns)

Carvin, Sophia and Thomas March married 26 Feb 1744 (the date should actually be written 26 Feb 1744/5; another entry in the parish register indicated Thomas Marsh and Sophia Corbin married 10 Feb 1745; the earlier date could have been their intention of marriage or publication of banns)

Carvin, William and Rachel Wright married 15 Aug 1745 (another entry in the parish register indicated William Corbin and Rachel Wright married 11 Aug 1745)

Casey, Henry, see "Henry Carey," q.v.

Castle, Sarah and Richard Burgis married -- Oct 1749 (another entry in the parish register indicated Richard Burgess and Sarah Caswell married 20 Aug 1749; the earlier date could have been their intention of marriage or publication of banns)

Caswell, Mary, daughter of Richard and Christian, born 3 Aug 1731 (her date of birth was mistakenly listed as 1 Aug in my 1987 book)

Caswell, Sarah, see "Sarah Castle," q.v.

Caswell, William, son of Richard and Christian, born 8 Dec 1726 (his date of birth was mistakenly listed as 7 Dec in my 1987 book)

Chainy, Sarah, see "Sarah Cheyne," q.v.

Chamberlain, Mary (Mrs.) and Henry Wetheral married 20 Dec 1722 (his name was listed as Witheral and at times as Witherall in the parish register; their marriage date was incompletely listed as 20 Dec 172- in my 1987 book)

Chamberlain, Susanna and Richard Tydings, both of Baltimore County, married 8 Aug 1797 (however, *Baltimore County Marriage Licenses, 1777-1798* indicated a license was issued to Richard Tydings and Susannah Hatton on 7 Aug 1797)

Chamberlaine, Cassandra and Charles Mulner married 7 Jan 1773 (her name was listed as Casander Chamberlane in my 1987 book)

Chamberlaine, Samuel and Elizabeth Pak't or Pakt married 24 Oct 1771 (their names were listed as Samuel Chamberlane and Elizabeth Pakt in my 1987 book and as Samuel Chamberlaine and Eliza. Pak't in *Maryland Marriages, 1634-1777*)

Chamberlaine, Susan and Abraham Standiford married 8 Oct 1769 (her name was mistakenly listed as Chaberlane in my 1987 book)

Chamberlin, Mary, see "Thomas Chamberlin," q.v.

Chamberlin, Thomas, son of Thomas and Mary, born 7 May 1717 (his name was misspelled as Charmbelin in my 1987 book)

Chambers, Thomas and Mary Fox married 6 Aug 1748 (another entry in the parish register indicated they married subsequent to 7 Jul 1748, but the exact date was not given, and her name was listed as Cox)

Chamney, Mary, see "Thomas Boswell," q.v.

Chance, William, son of Jeremiah and Wealthy Ann, born 28 Feb 1764 (his mother's name was misspelled as Wealthythy Ann in my 1987 book)

Chanley (Chamney), Mary and Thomas Boswell married -- May 1752 (the exact date was not given; another entry indicated Thomas Buswell and Mary Chamney married 30 Aug 1752; the earlier date could have been their intention of marriage or publication of banns, but is remains unclear whether or not these were two separate marriages)

Chapman, Sarah and Thomas Faurnan or Foreman married 4 Aug 1761 (his name was difficult to read in the parish register and it could have been Faurnan, Faurman or Foreman)

Cheney, Benjamin and Ruth Cheney married 23 Jun 1719 (this was listed in my 1987 book as Benjamin Chaeney and Ruth Chaeney married in June, 1719; *Maryland Marriages, 1634-1777* indicated they were married in Anne Arundel County on 23 Jun 1719; the name was also listed as Chainey in other parts of the parish register)

Cheney, Ruth and Benjamin Cheney married 23 Jun 1719 (this was listed in my 1987 book as Benjamin Chaeney and Ruth Chaeney married in June, 1719; *Maryland Marriages, 1634-1777* indicated they were married in Anne Arundel County on 23 Jun 1719; the name was also listed as Chainey in other parts of the parish register)

Cheney, Sarah, see "Sarah Chieney," q.v.

Chennerworth, John and Mary Smith married 26 Nov 1730 (the more common spellings of his name was Chenowith and Chinworth; although the date of marriage was entered in the parish register as 26 Nov 1730/31 this is incorrect because "double dating" applied only to dates from 1 Jan to 24 Mar in the old style calendar)

Cheshere, Cathrine and John Kingstone married 29 Apr 1754 (this marriage was inadvertently omitted from my 1987 book)

Cheshire, Elizabeth and John Sherelock married 30 Nov 1737 (her name was listed as Chesher in my 1987 book)

Cheverton, Sarah, see "Israel Parsley," q.v.

Cheyne, Permelie and John Owen married 12 Nov 1761 (her name was listed as Parmelie in my 1987 book)

Cheyne, Sarah and James Murphy married 9 Nov 1746 (another entry in the parish register indicated James Murphey and Sarah Chainy married 15 Dec

1746; the earlier date could have been their intention of marriage or publication of banns)

Cheyrton, Sarah and Israel Parsley married 5 Feb 1743 (the date should actually be written 5 Feb 1743/4; another entry in the parish register indicated Israel Pasley and Sarah Cheverton married 22 Jan 1744; the earlier date could have been their intention of marriage or publication of banns)

Chields, John, see "John Childs," q.v.

Chieney, Sarah and John Hatton married 17 May 1733 (his name was listed as Hatten and her surname as Chienie in my 1987 book)

Chilcoat, John and Providence Ensor married 24 Dec 1771 (his name was mistakenly listed as Gillcoat in the parish register)

Childs, John and Elizabeth Meads married 4 Dec 1743 (another entry in the parish register indicated John Chields and Elizabeth Mead married 17 Dec 1743; the earlier date could have been their intention of marriage or publication of banns)

Childs, John and Sarah Groves married 22 Jul 1752 (the entry in the parish register indicated they married subsequent to May, 1752, but the exact date was not given and her name was listed as Mary Groves)

Chilson, Walter and Hannah Martin married 16 Jun 1799 (the date was listed as 10 Jun 1799 in another part of the parish register; they were married by virtue of a license issued on 4 Jun 1799; his name was mistakenly listed as Chilsom in my 1987 book; *Maryland Marriages, 1778-1800* indicated the marriage date was 16 Jun 1799)

Chinworth, Thomas and Rachel Norris, both of Harford County, married 1 Jan 1788 (her last name was inadvertently omitted from my 1987 book)

Churchman, Enoch and Martha Norris, of Baltimore County, married 2 Feb 1792 (they were married by virtue of a license from Harford County as noted in the parish register; the license was issued on 1 Feb 1792)

Clagget, Rebecca and Edward Day married 19 Sep 1771 (her name was listed as Claggled or Claggett in my 1987 book)

Clarage (Clarager), Elizabeth and Bartholomew Flannagan married "in the month of September, 1750" (her name was listed as Elizabeth Clarage in my 1987 book, their names were listed as Bartholomew Flannagen and Eliza. Clarager in the parish register, and the marriage was entered among the 1756 marriages)

Clark, Elizabeth and John Harryman married 19 May 1752 (her name was listed as Clerk in my 1987 book)

Clark, George, see "Maria Clark," q.v.

Clark, James, see "James Clarke," q.v.

Clark, John and Cassandra Anderson, both of Harford County, married 15 Nov 1794 (the parish register indicated they were married by virtue of a license issued in Harford County, but no marriage license was found in Harford or Baltimore County)

Clark, John, see "Maria Clark," q.v.

Clark, Maria, daughter of John and Nancy, born 23 Mar 1797 (her father's name was mistakenly listed as George in my 1987 book)

Clark, Nancy, see "Maria Clark," q.v.

Clark, Sarah and Aquila Standiford married 27 Dec 1764 (his name was listed as Aqa. Standeford in the parish register)

Clark, Thomas and Cathrine Britain married 21 Nov 1749 (another entry in the parish register indicated Thomas Clerk and Kathrine Breton married between 24 Sep and 26 Nov 1749, but the exact date was not given)

Clarke, James and Margaret Plant married in 1753 (the complete date was not given in the parish register)

Clarke, James and Rachael Rock married 28 May 1769 (the exact date was not given, but their request to publish marriage banns was entered in the parish register and their names were listed as James Clark and Rachel Rock at that time)

Clarke, Martha and Peter Carroll married 7 Oct 1770 (his name was listed as Carrol in the parish register)

Clarke, Ruth and Walter Billingsley married 13 Feb 1772 (his name was listed as Billinsley in the parish register)

Clebedints, Michael and Cathrine Rozomister married 27 Mar 1763 (her name was difficult to read in the parish register and it was listed as Cath. Roza Mister or Cath. Rozamister since Cath. Roza was written on one line and mister was written on the next line)

Cleggett, Nicholas and Rebecca Young married 11 Feb 1768 (his name was listed as Nichs. and her name was listed as Reba. in the parish register)

Clerk, Elizabeth, see "Elizabeth Clark," q.v.

Clerk, Thomas, see "Thomas Clark," q.v.

Clyburn (Clybourn), Mary and Samuel Thornhill married 4 Feb 1747 (the date should actually be written 4 Feb 1747/8; another entry in the parish register indicated they married subsequent to 31 Jan 1748, but the exact date was not given)

Cock, William and Susannah Harriott married 18 Jun 1752 (her name was misspelled Susanhah in my 1987 book)

Coen, Rachel and Peter Bowles, both of Harford County, married 17 Jul 1788 (her name was mistakenly listed as Coon in my 1987 book)

Cole, Eddith and John Mallane married 8 Nov 1748 (another entry in the parish register indicated John Mallance and Ediff Cole married 6 Nov 1748)

Cole, Elizabeth, see "Zipporah Cole," q.v.

Cole, Thomas, see "Zipporah Cole," q.v.

Cole, William and Mary Stevens married 21 Nov 1742 (another entry in the parish register listed her name as Stephens and their marriage date as 16 Nov 1742; the earlier date could have been their intention of marriage or publication of banns)

Cole, Zipporah, daughter of Thomas and Elizabeth, born 17 Jan 1716 (her name was mistakenly listed as Leporah in my 1987 book)

Coleman, Charles and Lydia Forwood, both of Harford County, married 15 Mar 1791 (the marriage date was mistakenly listed as 17 Mar 1791 in my 1987 book; the parish register indicated they were married by virtue of a license from Harford County, but no marriage license was found in Harford or Baltimore County)

Coleman, John, see "John Grayham," q.v.

Colletson, Mary and Charles Green married 5 Jun 1753 (her name was mistakenly listed as Colletcon in my 1987 book)

Collett, Daniel and Susanna McKenly married 1 Aug 1749 (her name was listed as Susanah M'kenly in my 1987 book; another entry in the parish register indicated they married 14 May 1749; the earlier date could have been their intention of marriage or publication of banns)

Collins, George and Sarah Bailey, both of Baltimore County, married 26 Dec 1790 (although her name was listed as Bayley in the parish register, a marriage license issued 23 Dec 1790 listed her name as Bailey)

Collins, Lidie and John Palmer married 5 Nov 1769 (her name was listed as Sidie or Lidie in my 1987 book)

Collins, Martha and Charles Bennett married 11 Sep 1753 (another entry in the parish register indicated they married in 1753, but the exact date was not given and his name was listed as Bennet)

Collins, Sarah and James Woodland, both of Harford County, married 25 Dec 1792 (they were married by virtue of the publication of banns)

Collison, William and Susanna Adams married 3 Dec 1713 (their names were listed as William Collason and Susanah Addams in my 1987 book)

Colls, Rachael and Valentine Carback married 14 Sep 1769 (his name was mistakenly listed as Corback in my 1987 book)

Conden, Mary and Thomas Worrell, both of Baltimore County, married 12 May 1788 (his name was listed as Worrall in my 1987 book)

Condon, James and Mary Macnamara married 17 Apr 1765 (this marriage was entered in the parish register among the 1758 marriages)

Conelly, Artura and Elizabeth Parker married 17 Oct 1770 (her name was listed as Eliz. in the parish register)

Conn, Ann and Jesse Matthews, both of Harford County, married 1 Aug 1792 (they were married by virtue of a license issued on 30 Jul 1792; his name was listed as Mathews in the parish register)

Conn, Esther, see "Jane Conn," q.v.

Conn, Jane (Janett) and Arnold Rush, both of Harford County, married 27 Aug 1792 (the parish register indicated they were married by virtue of a license issued in Harford County on 25 Aug 1792, but no marriage license was found in Harford or Baltimore County; it is interesting to note that there was a marriage between Arnold Rush and Esther Conn in Harford County, but it was not until 1813)

Conner, John and Susanna Burgess married -- Aug 1744 (her name was listed as Susannah Burges in my 1987 book)

Conway, Morgan and Hannah Ruse married 12 Aug 1761 (her name was difficult to read in the parish register and it could have been Ruse or Rise)

Cook, Richard and Rebecca Murray married 9 Nov 1769 (her name was listed as Rebeca Murrey in my 1987 book)

Coop, Hannah, see "William Coop," q.v.

Coop, James, see "William Coop," q.v.

Coop, Richard and Hannah Stansbury married 6 Dec 1747 (another entry in the parish register indicated they married 10 Dec 1747 and his name was listed as Coup)

Coop, William, son of Hannah Coop, born 27 Apr 1790; James Coop, his Ba.(?) sponsor (this entry was inadvertently omitted from my 1987 book; the "Ba." written in the parish register is questionable and instead of "Ba." it may have been "Fa." to perhaps indicate father, but this is speculative)

Cooper, Sarah and William Everitt, both of Harford County, married 29 Mar 1795 (they were married by virtue of the publication of banns)

Copas (Capas), Mary and Robert Parker married 29 Nov 1762 (her name was difficult to read in the parish register and it could have been Copas or Capas)

Copass, John and Manerlin Wright married 24 Jan 1742 (the date should actually be written 24 Jan 1742/3; her name was mistakenly listed as Manuell in my 1987 book; another entry in the parish register listed his name as Copas and indicated they married 16 Jan 1742; the earlier date could have been their intention of marriage or publication of banns)

Copass, John, see "Mary Copass," q.v.

Copass, Manaley, see "Mary Copass," q.v.

Copass, Mary, daughter of John and Manaley, born 25 Dec 1743 (her surname was listed as Copas in the parish register and her mother's name was misspelled Manaby in my 1987 book; the name Manaley appeared to be a variation of, or a nickname for, Manerlin)

Cope, John and Mary Bush married 5 Feb 1748 (this marriage was entered in the parish register among the 1747 marriages and another entry in the parish register indicated they married subsequent to 31 Jan 1748, but the exact date was not given)

Cope, John and Brigitt Teate married 5 Feb 1753 (another entry in the parish register indicated marriage subsequent to November, 1752, but the exact date was not given; her name was listed as Bridget Tafe or Tate in *Maryland Marriages, 1634-1777* and in my 1987 book)

Copeland, Elizabeth and Sollomon Whealand married 18 Jan 1761 (his name was listed as Sollo. and her name was listed as Eliz. in the parish register)

Copperwhite, Susannah and William Keen married 21 Nov 1757 (her last name was difficult to read in the parish register and it could have been Copperwhite or Crosswhite?; her first name was listed as Sushannah in the parish register, but was misspelled as Sishannah in my 1987 book)

Corbin, Dinah and Richard Wiat married 10 May 1772 (his name was mistakenly listed as Wist in my 1987 book)

Corbin, Elizabeth and Edmund Deadman married 20 Jan 1753 (another entry in the parish register indicated they married in 1753, but the exact date was not given and her name was listed as Eliza. Corben)

Corbin, Leah and Laban Welch married 3 Sep 1761 (his name could have been Welch or Welsh in the parish register)

Corbin, Providence and Henry Perigoe married 14 Jan 1745 (the date should actually be written 14 Jan 1745/6; another entry in the parish register indicated they married 24 Nov 1745; the earlier date could have been their intention of marriage or publication of banns)

Corbin, Sophia, see "Sophia Carvin," q.v.

Corbin, Unity and Robert Green married 21 Sep 1746 (another entry in the parish register indicated they married 25 Sep 1746)

Corbin, William, see "William Carvin," q.v.

Cord, Elizabeth (of Baltimore County) and Thomas Johnson (of Harford County) married 17 Jun 1792 (they were married by virtue of a license issued in Baltimore County on 15 Jun 1792; his name was listed as Johnston in another part of the parish register, but it was listed as Johnson on the marriage license)

Cordsman, Philip and Anne Brooks married in 1753 (the complete date was not given in the parish register)

Cosley, James and Mary Hill married 3 Jan 1744 (another entry in the parish register indicated they married some time between 25 Dec 1744 and 28 Jan 1745, but the exact date was not given; his name was also listed as Costley)

Costley, Martha and William Ensor married 4 Sep 1766 (his name was listed as Wm. Enzor in the parish register and mistakenly listed as Enzoe in my 1987 book)

Cotterel, John and Sarah Raven married 10 Mar 1763 (her name was listed as Reaven in the parish register)

Cotterrel, John and Ann Wood married 14 Jun 1752 (another entry in the parish register indicated John Cotrall and Anne Wood married subsequent to May 1752, but the exact date was not given)

Cottrall, Thomas and Frances Milhughs married 31 Jul 1743 (her name was mistakenly listed as Williams in my 1987 book; another entry in the parish register indicated their names were Thomas Cotteraell and Frances Milhuse and they married 4 Aug 1743; their names were listed as Thomas Cotterel and Frances Millhughes in *Maryland Marriages, 1634-1777*)

Coudry, Anne and Thomas Durbin married -- Jan 1737 (her name was listed as Condry in my 1987 book and as Cowdrey in *Baltimore County Families, 1659-1759*, but this marriage was not listed in *Maryland Marriages, 1634-1777*)

Cowan, Dunham and Mary Taylor married 21 -- 1768 (probably married 21 Sep 1768, but the information was incomplete in the parish register)

Cowan, Mary and John Middleton, both of Harford County, married 15 Sep 1793 (they were married by virtue of a license issued on 28 Aug 1793)

Cowdry, Mary and Patrick Whealand married 26 Jan 1749 (the date should actually be 26 Jan 1740/50; another entry in the parish register indicated they married some time between 17 Dec 1749 and 11 Feb 1750, but the exact date was not given; her name was mistakenly listed as Candry in my 1987 book)

Cowen, Leonard and Mary Fowler, both of Harford County, married 15 May 1791 (they were married by virtue of the publication of banns)

Cox, Jacob, see "Thomas Cox," q.v.

Cox, John and Elizabeth Sympson married 30 Nov 1742 (her name was listed as Eliz. Simpson in *Maryland Marriages, 1634-1777*)

Cox, Mary, see "Mary Fox," q.v.

Cox, Susannah and John Low married 29 Mar 1744 (another entry in the parish register indicated they married 26 Mar 1744)

Cox, Thomas and Elizabeth Gaine married 13 Dec 1744 (another entry in the parish register indicated Jacob Cox and Elizabeth Gain married on this date)

Crabtree, Samuel, son of William, born 25 Jul 1725 (although his date of birth was listed as 25 Jul 17-- in my 1987 book, it was noted as 25 Jul 1725 in *Baltimore County Families, 1659-1759*)

Crabtree, William, see "Samuel Crabtree," q.v.

Crawford, Margaret and Benjamin Wilmer married 29 May 1800 (they were married by virtue of a license issued on 28 May 1800)

Crawford, Mordicai and Susannah Tucker married 16 Sep 1750 (her name was mistakenly listed as Suhannah in my 1987 book)

Craws, Michael and Sarah Hanson, both of Harford County, married 28 Feb 1788 (her name was mistakenly listed as Hauson in my 1987 book)

Crockett, John and Ann Hixson married 25 Dec 1744 (another entry in the parish register indicated John Crokat and Anne Hickson married on this date while another entry misspelled her name was Fixson)

Cromwell, Richard (of Anne Arundel County) and Mary Owings (of Baltimore County) married 6 Feb 1800 (this information was omitted from my 1987 book)

Crook, Elizabeth and Aquila Hatten married 29 Dec 1767 (this marriage was inadvertently omitted from my 1987 book)

Cross, Richard and Tabitha Hicks married 1 Jan 1761 (her name was listed as Tab. Hixs in the parish register and in my 1987 book)

Crouch, Thomas and Elizabeth McGowan, both of Harford County, married 27 Dec 1790 (although his name was listed as Groush or Gorush in another part of the parish register and they were married by license, no marriage license was found in Harford or Baltimore County; the name was listed as Crouch in my 1987 book and in *Maryland Marriages, 1778-1800*)

Crutchinton, George and Ann Baker married 16 Jun 1768 (her name looked like Ann Bakr. in the parish register)

Cullison, Elizabeth, see "Absolom Gadd," q.v.

Cunningham, Daniel and Ann Amos, both of Harford County, married 19 Oct 1797 (her name was listed as Anna in another part of the parish register; they were married by virtue of a license issued on 16 Oct 1797 which listed her name as Amoss)

Cunningham, Hugh and Mary Acre married in 1749 (the exact date was not given in the parish register, but apparently they married some time between 26 Mar and 14 May 1749; his name was listed as Cuninghame)

Cunningham, William and Margarett Brierly married ---- (no date was given, but the marriage appeared between entries made on 29 Dec and 31 Dec 1761 in the parish register; his name was listed as Wm. Cuninggam)

Curle, William and Elizabeth Ward married in 1775 (the exact date of marriage was not given, but their request to publish marriage banns was dated 10 Aug 1775 in the parish register)

Curry, Mary and Samuel McMath, both of Harford County, married 19 Jun 1792 (they were married by virtue of the publication of banns; the marriage date was mistakenly listed as 18 Jun 1792 in my 1987 book and her name was mistakenly listed as Cussy in another part of the parish register)

Cutchin, Beging, son of Robert and Winiford, born 22 Jan 1732 (his first name was listed as Begging and Bigging in *Baltimore County Families, 1659-1759*)

Cutchin, Mary and Benjamin Ricketts married 2 Jun 1759 (this marriage was entered in the parish register among the 1758 marriages)

Cutchin, Robert and Winiford Breavinton married 20 Apr 1731 (her name was listed as Brewenton in my 1987 book and as Breavinton in *Baltimore County Families, 1659-1759*)

Cutchin, Robert, see "Beging Cutchin," q.v.

Cutchin, Thomas and Mary Gott married 5 Dec 1743 (another entry in the parish register indicated they married 27 Nov 1743 and his name was listed as Gudgins; the earlier date could have been their intention of marriage or publication of banns)

Cutchin, Winiford, see "Beging Cutchin," q.v.

Dallerhide, Providence and John Frissell married 25 Oct 1722 (they were mistakenly listed as John Frissil and Providence Dallatude married -- Nov 1721 in another part of the parish register and in my 1987 book)

Dallerhide, Sarah and William Denton married 27 Feb 1725 (her name was mistakenly listed as Dallerbride in my 1987 book)

Dallerhyde, Sarah and Thomas Armstrong married 28 Dec 1752 (another entry in the parish register indicated they married in 1752, but the exact date was not given, and her name was listed as Dellerhide)

Danbie, Elizabeth and John Parker married 1 Jan 1739 (another entry in the parish register indicated John Parker and Mary Danbe married on this date)

Darymple, ---- and Sarah Braser married in summer of 1742 "in the forest" (*Maryland Marriages, 1634-1777* listed it as "(?) Darumple married Sarah Braser, no date given")

Daugh, Willyahnah, daughter of William and Ann, born 7 Mar 1740 (her name was listed as Willyalmah in *Baltimore County Families, 1659-1759*)

Davies, Rebecca and Nathan Phipps, both of Harford County, married 29 Jan 1789 (his name was listed as Phips in my 1987 book)

Davinn, Thomas and Ann Harryman married 10 Sep 1771 (her name was mistakenly listed as Harmpmann in my 1987 book)

Dawney, Henry and Martha Hill married 12 Sep 1799 (they were married by virtue of a license issued on 10 Sep 1799)

Dawney, James, see "James Dorney," q.v.

Daws, Edward and Ann Grunden, both of Harford County, married 29 Dec 1793 (they were married by virtue of a license issued on 27 Dec 1793)

Dawson, Mary and Dennis McLaughlin, both of Baltimore County, married 18 Dec 1787 (her name was mistakenly listed as Rachel Norris in my 1987 book)

Day, Avarilla, see "Nicholas Day," q.v.

Day, Edward and Rebecca Clagget married 19 Sep 1771 (her name was listed as Claggled or Claggett in my 1987 book)

Day, Edward, see "Nicholas Day" and "John Day," q.v.

Day, Elizabeth and Alexander McComas married 19 Nov 1713 (his name was listed as Elecksander Mecomas in my 1987 book)

Day, Hezekiah and Alce Bonney married 12 Jul 1713 (her maiden name was mistakenly listed as Alce Bonney Day in my 1987 book)

Day, John (son of Edward) and Sarah York married 30 Dec 1764 (another entry in the parish register indicated they were married about 4 o'clock in the afternoon)

Day, John, see "Young Day," q.v.

Day, Letitia, see "Pamala Day," q.v.

Day, Michael, see "Nicholas Day," q.v.

Day, Nicholas, son of Edward and Avarilla, born 19 Jan 1732 (his name was mistakenly listed as Michael instead of Nicholas in my 1987 book)

Day, Pamala, daughter of William Fell and Letitia, born 1791, baptized 16 Jun 1793 (her date of birth was listed as 20 Mar 1792 in my 1987 book and the date of baptism was omitted)

Day, William Fell, see "Pamala Day," q.v.

Day, Young, child of John and ----, born ----, baptized 8 Jun 1794 (the date of birth was not given in the parish register and the baptism date was inadvertently omitted from my 1987 book)

Deadman, Edmund and Elizabeth Corbin married 20 Jan 1753 (another entry in the parish register indicated they married in 1753, but the exact date was not given and her name was listed as Eliza. Corben)

Deadman, Thomas and Sarah Griffith married 2 Oct 1749 (another entry in the parish register indicated they married 24 Sep 1749 and her name was listed as Griffin; the earlier date could have been their intention of marriage or publication of banns)

Deans, Hugh, see "John Mercer," q.v.

Deason, Alimsway, daughter of William and Ann, born 20 or 28 Dec 1747 (her name was listed as Alimessey in my 1987 book, but her last name was inadvertantly omitted; her date of birth was unclear in the parish register and could be 20 or 28 Dec 1747; *Baltimore County Families, 1659-1759* listed her name as Alimsway, born 28 Dec 1747)

Deason, Ann, see "Alimsway Deason," q.v.

Deason, Benjamin and Tarrisha Shepard married 9 Dec 1742 (another entry in the parish register indicated Benjamin Deason and ---- Shepard, both of this parish, married 21 Nov 1742; the earlier date could have been their intention of marriage or publication of banns)

Deason, Jemima and John Rockhold married 14 Jul 1771 (her name was listed as Deeson in the parish register)

Deason, John and Mary Hall married 1 May 1749 (another entry in the parish register indicated they married between 26 Mar 1749 and 14 May 1749, but the exact date was not given)

Deason, Joseph and Ketura(h) Hall married 23 Nov 1746 (another entry in the parish register indicated they married 27 Nov 1746)

Deason, Margaret and Nathan Frissel married 18 Apr 1751 (another entry in the parish register indicated they married in 1751, but the exact date was not given, and his name was listed as Frizell)

Deason, Rebecca and William Standiford, Jr. married 27 May 1767 (her name was listed as Reb. in the parish register and his name was listed as Wm. Standeford Jnr.)

Deason, Sarah and William Hudson married 30 Jan 1749 (the date should actually be 30 Jan 1749/50; another entry in the parish register indicated they married subsequent to 17 Dec 1749, but the exact date was not given)

Deason, William, see "Alimsway Deason," q.v.

Deaver, Ann and George Stolinger married 23 Jan 1800 (her name was mistakenly listed as Doover in my 1987 book)

Debrular, George and Araminta Nutterville, both of Harford County, married 12 Jul 1791 (although her name looked like Aminta Nutterwell in the parish register, a marriage license issued 11 Jul 1791 listed their names as George Debruler and Aramenta Nutterville)

Debrular, Greenberry and Rachel Henley married 23 May 1799 (they were married by virtue of a license issued that same day; her name was misspelled Healey in another part of the parish register)

Deegan, Patrick and Polly McComas married 24 Oct 1799 (they were married by virtue of a license issued on 23 Oct 1799; his name was mistakenly listed as Dargay in my 1987 book, but it was listed as Deegan in another part of that book)

Degue, Anthony son(?) and Elizabeth Downs married 23 May 1753 (his most unusual name was written in the parish register as either Anthony son Degue or Anthonyson Degue and it remains an identification problem)

Delevit, Peter and Ann Jones, both of Baltimore County, married 16 Feb 1794 (his name was listed as Delivett in my 1987 book, but it was also listed as Delevit in the parish register and as Delevet when the marriage license was issued on 12 Feb 1794)

Demmet, Sarah and Joseph Boram married 7 Aug 1753 (another entry in the parish register indicated Joseph Barham and Sarah Demmett married in 1753, but the exact date was not given)

Demmett, William (son of William) and Dorothy Swan married 14 Dec 1765 (another entry in the parish register indicated William Demmett and Dorthy Swan married 13 Dec 1765; information in my 1987 book was incorrect in stating that William Demmett, son of William Demmett and Dorothy Swan, was born 14 Dec 1765)

Demmitt, Elizabeth, see "William Demmitt," q.v.

Demmitt, James and Barbara Broad married 27 Mar 1723 (his name was listed as Demmett and her first name was misspelled as Barbaro in my 1987 book)

Demmitt, John and Frances White married 5 Aug 1759 (her name was difficult to read in the parish register and it could have been White or Waits)

Demmitt, William, son of William and Elizabeth, born 1 Jun 1715 (his name was listed as Demitt or Dernit in my 1987 book)

Demmitt, William Jr. and Cathrene Warden Bull married 6 Oct 1736 (his name was listed without the Jr. in my 1987 book)

Demorse, Eliner and James Hope married 24 May 1768 (her name was listed as Demorce in the parish register)

Demorse, John and Susannah Ramsey married 2 Feb 1743 (the date should actually be written 2 Feb 1743/4; his name was listed as Demoss in other parts of the parish register; another entry in the parish register indicated John Demors of Opecan and Susanna Ramsey of this parish married 1 Jan 1744; the earlier date could have been their intention of marriage or publication of banns)

Demorse, Katherine and Thomas Gibson married 22 Dec 1761 (her name was listed as Kathrine Demorce in the parish register)

Demorse, Lewes and Margrett Ramsey married 6 Jan 1743 (the date should actually be written 6 Jan 1743/4; another entry in the parish register indicated Lewis Demors of Opecan and Margaret Ramsey of this parish married 1 Jan 1744; his name was listed as Demoss in other parts of the parish register)

Dennock, Mary and Francis Poulson married 13 Feb 1749 (the date should actually be written 13 Feb 1748/9; another entry in the parish register indicated Francis Polson and Mary Dennick married some time between November 1748 and February 1749, but the exact date was not given)

Denton, William and Sarah Dallerhide married 27 Feb 1725 (her name was mistakenly listed as Dallerbride in my 1987 book)

Dew, Robert and Esther Raven married 3 Oct 1754 (her name was listed as Easther Reaven in the parish register)

Ditto, Christian and Thomas Gadd married 21 Jan 1733 (another entry in the parish register indicated they married 22 Jan 1732/3)

Divers, Sarah and John Lucas, both of Baltimore County, married 7 Feb 1793 (her name was listed as Divins in *Maryland Marriages, 1778-1800* and as Divies in another part of the parish register; her name was listed as Divers in my 1987 book and also on their marriage license issued on 22 Jan 1793)

Dives, Christopher and Frances Hill married 10 Dec 1728 (his name was listed as Divas in the parish register and also in my 1987 book, but the more common spellings of the name were Dives or Divers; it was mistakenly listed as Davis in *Maryland Marriages, 1634-1777*)

Dives, Christopher and Sarah Nixon married 24 Jun 1762 (his first name was listed as Chris. in the parish register; her last name was difficult to read and could have been Nixon, Nixion or Minson)

Dobson, James and Jane Montgomery married 1 Jul 1745 (another entry in the parish register indicated they married 23 Jun 1745 and listed her name as Mongumry)

Doddridge, Lettice and George York married 7 May 1721 (her name was listed as Dawdridge in my 1987 book)

Doddridge, William, see "William Dortridge," q.v.

Donovan, Ephraim and Charlotte Taylor, both of Harford County, married 28 Mar 1791 (his name was listed as Donavon in the parish register)

Dorney, Ann(e) and William Yeates married 28 Apr 1748 (another entry in the parish register indicated William Yates and Anne Dorney married 24 Apr 1748)

Dorney, Anne and Edward York married 21 Oct 1742 (another entry in the parish register indicated they married 26 Sep 1742; the earlier date could have been their intention of marriage or publication of banns)

Dorney, James and Mary Yeats married 14 Dec 1743 (another entry in the parish register indicated they married 20 Nov 1743 and his name was listed as Dawney; the earlier date could have been their intention of marriage or publication of banns)

Dorney, James and Ann Cadle married 9 Aug 1749 (another entry in the parish register indicated they married some time in May 1749 and spelled her name Caddle; the earlier date could have been their intention of marriage or publication of banns)

Dorney, Sarah and John Thrift married "in the year 1732" (this marriage was entered in the parish register among the 1752 marriages)

Dorsey, Edward, see "Henry Dorsey," q.v.

Dorsey, Henry (son of Edward) and Elizabeth Smithson, both of Harford County, married 5 Feb 1795 (they were married by virtue of a license issued in Harford County on that same day)

Dorsey, John and Martha Woodland married 18 Dec 1770 (their names were listed as John Dorcey and Marth Woodland in my 1987 book)

Dorsey, John Hammond and Ann Maxwell married 20 Jan 1772 (his middle name was listed as Hammon in the parish register)

Dorsey, Rebecca and John Lane married 6 -- 1768 (probably married 6 Oct 1768, but the information was incomplete in the parish register)

Dortridge, William and Margret Murphy married 19 Oct 1749 (another entry in the parish register indicated William Dawdrege and Margaret Murphey married 3 Sep 1749; the earlier date could have been their intention of marriage or publication of banns)

Doubty, Sarah, daughter of Thomas and Luraner, born 17 Apr 1761, died -- Feb 1762 (her mother's name was misspelled Lurauer in my 1987 book)

Downs, Elizabeth and Anthony son Degue married 23 May 1753 (his most unusual name was written in the parish register as either Anthony son Degue or Anthonyson Degue and it remains an identification problem)

Downs, Henry and Deleah Enlows married 10 Aug 1790 (this marriage was inadvertently omitted from my 1987 book and her name was written as Deleast in another part of the parish register)

Downs, Mary and John Huggins, Jr. married 7 Oct 1742 (another entry in the parish register indicated John Hugins and Mary Downes married 29 Aug 1742; the earlier date could have been their intention of marriage or publication of banns)

Doyle, Elizabeth and James Cain married 30 Dec 1744 (another entry in the parish register indicated they married 25 Dec 1744)

Druley, Elizabeth and Henry Smith married -- Jun 1738 (this same information was listed in *Maryland Marriages, 1634-1777* which also indicated Henry Smith and Eliz. Dury married 6 Jun 1738 in Talbot County)

Dukes, Pemela and John Pickett married 3 Oct 1756 (his name was listed as Jno. in the parish register and her name was listed as Pemela or Pernela in my 1987 book)

Dunham, Thomas, see "Thomas Durham," q.v.

Dunnock, John and Mary Pasmore married 16 Jan 1743 (the date should actually be written 16 Jan 1742/3; his name was mistakenly listed as Dannock and her name as Palmore in my 1987 book; another entry in the parish register indicated John Dunnike and Mary Pasmore married 5 Dec 1742; the earlier date could have been their intention of marriage or publication of banns)

Durbin, Dricella and James Nicholson married 24 Dec 1757 (her name was mistakenly listed as Ducella in my 1987 book)

Durbin, John and Abarillah Scott married 20 Aug 1715 (their names were listed as John Derbin and Abrillah Scott in my 1987 book)

Durbin, John and Eleanor Odean married 13 Dec 1743 (her name was listed as Elioner Odan in *Maryland Marriages, 1634-1777*)

Durbin, Thomas and Anne Coudry married -- Jan 1737 (her name was listed as Condry in my 1987 book and as Cowdrey in *Baltimore County Families, 1659-1759*, but this marriage was not listed in *Maryland Marriages, 1634-1777*)

Durham (Durban), Nancy and Moses Taylor, both of Harford County, married 27 Dec 1792 (her name was listed as Durban in another part of the parish register; no marriage license was found in Baltimore or Harford County to verify the spelling of her name because they were married by virtue of the publication of banns)

Durham, Eleanor, see "James Durham" and "John Durham" and "Samuel Durham" and "Sarah Durham," q.v.

Durham, James, son of Samuel and Eleanor, born 1 Jan 1728 (although his name was mistakenly listed as Darram and his year of birth as 172- in my 1987 book, he was noted as James Durham, born 1 Jan 1728, in *Baltimore County Families, 1659-1759*)

Durham, James and Rebeckah Anderson married 12 Feb 1720 (her first name was misspelled Reneckah in my 1987 book)

Durham, John, son of Samuel and Eleanor, born 8 Oct 1723 (his name was misspelled as Durrma in my 1987 book)

Durham, Samuel, son of Samuel and Eleanor, born 18 Feb 1726/7 (his name was mistakenly listed as Darram in my 1987 book)

Durham, Samuel and Eleanor Smithson married 15 Jan 1723 (this was listed as Samuel Durram and Elinor Smithson married 15 Jan 17-- in my 1987 book)

Durham, Samuel, see "James Durham" and "John Durham" and "Sarah Durham," q.v.

Durham, Sarah, daughter of Samuel and Eleanor, born 2 Jun 1725 (her name was mistakenly listed as Darram in my 1987 book)

Durham, Susanna and Alexander Hillen married 16 May 1799 (they were married by virtue of a license issued that same day; his name was listed as Hellen in another part of the parish register)

Durham, Thomas and Rachel Shoudy, both of Harford County, married 20 Feb 1791 (they were married by virtue of the publication of banns; her name was listed as Shondy or Shoudy in my 1987 book and the marriage date was mistakenly listed as 15 Mar 1791; his name was listed as Dunham in another part of the parish register)

Durham, Zacharias and Lucia Husband, both of Harford County, married 11 Mar 1792 (they were married by virtue of the publication of banns)

Dury, Eliz., see "Elizabeth Druley," q.v.

Duwaull, ---- and Isaac Burns married 31 Mar 1761 (her first name was not indicated in the parish register)

Earl, Elizabeth and Peter Golden married 15 Nov 1742 (his name was listed as Golding in other parts of the parish register and another entry in the parish register indicated they married 10 Oct 1742; the earlier date could have been their intention of marriage or publication of banns)

Eddee, Jonathan and Rebecca York married 4 Apr 1743 (his name was listed as Edy and Ady in other parts of the parish register and another entry in the parish register indicated Jonathan Ady and Rebeccah York married 27 Mar 1743; the earlier date could have been their intention of marriage or publication of banns)

Edey, William and Cloe Standiford married 22 Nov 1770 (his name was listed as Edye in my 1987 book)

Edwards, Edward and Cassandra Beard married 1 Apr 1762 (her name was listed as Cas. in the parish register)

Edwards, Temperance and Benjamin Tracy married 13 May 1770 (their names were actually listed as Benn Trasy and Tempy Edwards in the parish register)

Edwards, William and Jane Broad married 17 Sep 1748 (another entry in the parish register indicated they married subsequent to 4 Sep 1748, but the exact date was not given)

Eights, Sarah and James Blunden married 1 Dec 1759 (his name was mistakenly listed as Blunder in my 1987 book)

Ellender, George and Sarah Grimes, both of Baltimore County, married 12 Feb 1792 (his name was listed as Ellinder in my 1987 book; they were married by virtue of a license from Baltimore County as noted in the parish register; the license was issued on 10 Feb 1792 and listed his name as Elender)

Ellender, George, see "Nicholas Grimes Ellender" and "Joshua Ellender," q.v.

Ellender, Joshua, son of George and Sarah, born 26 Apr 1795 (his name was listed as Ellinder in my 1987 book)

Ellender, Joshua, age about 18 months, buried 7 Jun 1797 with his brother Solomon (his last name was listed as Ellinor instead of Ellender in my 1987 book)

Ellender, Nicholas Grimes, son of George and Sarah, born 20 Apr 1793 (his name was also listed as Nickey Grimes Ellinder in the parish register)

Ellender, Sarah, see "Nicholas Grimes Ellender" and "Joshua Ellender," q.v.

Ellender, Solomon, age 2 months, buried 7 Jun 1797 with his brother Joshua (his name was listed as Ellinor instead of Ellender in my 1987 book)

Ellenor (Ellender), William and Barbara Bremer, both of Baltimore County, married 19 Feb 1795 (although his last name was listed as Ellenor in the parish register, it could have been Ellender; her name was mistakenly listed as Bemer in my 1987 book and as Bemer or Berner in *Maryland Marriages, 1778-1800*; however, no license was found in Baltimore or Harford County in order to verify the spelling of the names)

Elliott, John and Elizabeth Wright married 22 Dec 1761 (the date of marriage was mistakenly listed as 23 Dec in my 1987 book)

Elliott, Marberril and Jemima Standiford married 13 Jan 1756 (their names were listed in the parish register as "Marberril, Elliott & Jemima Standeford")

Elliott, Mary and Henry Enloes married 26 May 1763 (her name was listed as Ellcott in my 1987 book)

Elliott, Philip Lock and Sarah Sparks married 3 Sep 1762 (his name was listed as Phill. Lock Elliott in the parish register and mistakenly listed as Phill. Lock Ellcott in my 1987 book and in *Maryland Marriages, 1634-1777*; his correct full name was Philip Lock Elliott as noted in William Wright's admin. account in 1750)

Elliott, Sarah and James Poor married in 1747 (the complete date was not given in the parish register and her name was spelled Elliot in my 1987 book)

Elliott, William and Karran Johnson married 17 May 1740 (this marriage was entered in the parish register among the 1752 marriages)

Ellwood, Richard and Mary Linzey married 9 Oct 1748 (another entry in the parish register listed her name as Lindsay; she was mistakenly listed as Sinzey in my 1987 book)

Ellwood, Sarah and William Williams married 8 Dec 1748 (another entry in the parish register indicated they married in December 1748, but the day was not given)

Emes, John and Elizabeth Stiles married -- Sep 1749 (the exact date was not given, but it was apparently some time between 3 Sep and 24 Sep 1749)

Enloes, Henry and Mary Elliott married 26 May 1763 (her name was listed as Ellcott in my 1987 book)

Enloes, Prudence, see "James Marsh Enlow (Enloes)," q.v.

Enlow (Enlowe), Elizabeth and Thomas Weekes or Weeks married 12 Dec 1742 (another entry in the parish register indicated Thomas Wicks and Elizabeth Enlow married 15 Dec 1742)

Enlow (Enloes), James Marsh, son of James and Prudence, born 20 Apr 1790 (the name Enlow looked like Enloes in the parish register, but the marriage of his parents was not found in county marriage licenses in order to verify the spelling)

Enlows, Deleah and Henry Downs married 10 Aug 1790 (this marriage was inadvertently omitted from my 1987 book and her name was written as Deleast in another part of the parish register)

Ensor, James, son of Thomas and Mary, born 23 Aug 1746 (his name was listed as Enzer in my 1987 book)

Ensor, John and Dorcas Gorsuch married 2 Jul 1772 (her name was mistakenly listed as Gorsich in my 1987 book)

Ensor, Mary, see "James Ensor," q.v.

Ensor, Providence and John Chilcoat married 24 Dec 1771 (his name was mistakenly listed as Gillcoat in the parish register)

Ensor, Thomas, see "James Ensor," q.v.

Ensor, William and Martha Costley married 4 Sep 1766 (his name was listed as Wm. Enzor in the parish register and mistakenly listed as Enzoe in my 1987 book)

Erickson, Elizabeth and Nicholas Power married 6 Jan 1753 (his name was listed in the parish register as Nichs. Poor, but subsequent research indicated his name was actually Nicholas Power)

Evans, Anne and John Bradley married 2 Oct 1743 (another entry in the parish register indicated they married 4 Sep 1743 and listed her name as Evens; the earlier date could have been their intention of marriage or publication of banns)

Evans, Robert and Ann Barton married 22 Aug 1771 (their names were listed as Robert Evins and Ann Bartinn in the parish register)

Everett (Everitt), John and Elizabeth Jackman married 5 May 1771 (their names were listed as John Everat and Eliz. Jackman in the parish register)

Everett (Everitt), Mary and Francis Norrington married 19 Feb 1749 (another entry in the parish register indicated they married subsequent to 11 Feb 1750, but the exact date was not given)

Everett (Everitt), William and Sarah Cooper, both of Harford County, married 29 Mar 1795 (they were married by virtue of the publication of banns)

Fairchild, Edward and Margery Bringingham married 6 Dec 1761 (her name was listed as Margarey in my 1987 book)

Fara, Isabell, see "Elizabeth Finer," q.v.

Farlow (Harlow?), Elianor and Abraham Ristone married 11 Nov 1762 (her name was difficult to read in the parish register and could have been Farlow or Harlow)

Faurnan (Faurman?), Thomas and Sarah Chapman married 4 Aug 1761 (his name was difficult to read in the parish register and it could have been Faurnan, Faurman or Foreman)

Felin, Edward and Mary Linsey married in 1748 (the exact date of marriage was not given, but the entry in the parish register indicated they married subsequent to 31 Jan 1748; *Maryland Marriages, 1634-1777* listed the marriage as "Edward Flin and Mary Linsey, 1748")

Fell, Mary and John Benkin married 9 Feb 1765 (his name in the parish register could be either Jno. Benkin, Binkin or Burkin)

Felton, Abraham, see "Abraham Hilton," q.v.

Feluallen (Flualler), Elizabeth and Richard Green married 2 Sep 1743 (her name was listed as Flualler in *Maryland Marriages, 1634-1777* and was misspelled as Henallen in my 1987 book; another entry in the parish register indicated they married 31 Jul 1743; the earlier date could have been their intention of marriage or publication of banns)

Fields, Anne and Isaac Ward married in 1753 (the complete date was not given in the parish register)

Finagan, Ariana, see "Aranea Slemaker," q.v.

Finer, Elizabeth and William Miver married 10 Oct 1748 (another entry in the parish register indicated William Miver and Isabell Fara married 4 Sep 1748; the earlier date could have been their intention of marriage or publication of banns; *Maryland Marriages, 1634-1777* listed them as two separate marriages)

Finnagan, Henry Patrick and Aranea Slemaker, both of Harford County, married 26 Apr 1792 (her name was mistakenly listed as Aransa Demaker in my 1987 book and the marriage date was mistakenly listed as 17 Jun 1792; they were married by virtue of a license issued on 25 Apr 1792 which listed their names as H. Patrick Finnagan and Areanea Slemaker; there was a subsequent license for Ariana Finagan and John Renaud issued on 25 Aug 1796 in Harford County)

Fixson, Ann, see "Ann Hickson (Hixson)," q.v.

Flanagan, Achsah, see "John Holliday Flanagan," q.v.

Flanagan, Edward, see "Maria Flanagan" and "John Holliday Flanagan," q.v.

Flanagan, Elizabeth, see "Maria Flanagan" and "John Holliday Flanagan," q.v.

Flanagan, Elizabeth and Zenas Wells married 5 Sep 1799 (his name was mistakenly listed once as Thomas in my 1987 book and then as Zenas in another part of that book; their marriage license was issued 4 Sep 1799; *Maryland Marriages, 1634-1777* first listed her name as Hanazan and then indicated Flanagan)

Flanagan, John Holliday and Achsah Holliday Flanagan, twins of Edward and Elizabeth, born 23 Jul 1792 (the date was listed as 22 Jul 1792 in my 1987 book and her name was mistakenly listed as Nesah instead of Achsah)

Flanagan, Maria, daughter of Edward and Elizabeth, born 8 Jun 1789 (her name was mistakenly listed as Marion in my 1987 book)

Flannagan, Bartholomew and Elizabeth Clarage or Clarager married "in the month of September, 1750" (her name was listed as Elizabeth Clarage in my 1987 book; their names were listed as Bartholomew Flannagen and Eliza. Clarager in the parish register and their marriage was entered among the 1756 marriages)

Flannagan, Mary and Thomas Rooke married 6 Nov 1770 (her name was listed as Flannagin in *Maryland Marriages, 1634-1777* and mistakenly listed as Flanngin in my 1987 book)

Flannen, Francis and Sarah Whealand married 2 Oct 1748 (another entry in the parish register indicated Francis Flannel and Sarah Whaland married subsequent to 4 Sep 1748, but the exact date was not given)

Fleming, William and Mary Jane married 5 Nov 1759 (her last name was difficult to read in the parish register, but it could have been Jane or Jasie)

Fleury, Paul Aimé and Clara Young, both of Baltimore County, married 28 Oct 1794 (his name was listed as Paul Aimee Fleury and her name as Clare

Young in another part of the parish register; marriage license was issued to
Mr. Fleury and Clara Young on 11 Oct 1794)

Flin, Edward, see "Edward Felin," q.v.

Flincham, Sarah, age 4 years old, resident of Harford County, buried 9 Dec 1792
(her name was listed as Sarah Flindam in my 1987 book)

Ford, Mary (of Baltimore County) and Joshua Ady (of Harford County) married
6 Nov 1792 (the parish register indicated they were married by virtue of a
license issued in Baltimore County, but no marriage license was found in
Baltimore or Harford County)

Foreasay, Peter and Ann Axter married 4 Nov 1758 (his name was difficult to
read in the parish register and it could have been Foreasey or Forcasey)

Foreasjute, Ann and John Welcher married 24 Apr 1764 (her last name was
most unusual and difficult to read in the parish register)

Foreman, Thomas, see "Thomas Faurnan," q.v.

Forrest, Ann(e) and James Mead (son of Edward) married 21 Dec 1747 (another
entry in the parish register indicated James Meads and Anne Forrest married
some time between 6 Dec 1747 and 3 Jan 1748, but the exact date was not
given)

Forrord (Porrord?), Mary and Devans Scotter married 9 Jul 1761 (her name was
difficult to read in the parish register and it could have been Forrord or
Porrord)

Forwood, Lydia and Charles Coleman, both of Harford County, married 15 Mar
1791 (the marriage date was mistakenly listed as 17 Mar 1791 in my 1987
book; the parish register indicated they were married by virtue of a license
from Harford County, but no marriage license was found in Harford or
Baltimore County)

Foster, Samuel and Margrett Gaton or Guton married 26 Feb 1749 (another
entry in the parish register indicated they married subsequent to 11 Feb
1750, but the exact date was not given, and her name was listed as Margaret
Guiton)

Fowler, Mary and Leonard Cowen, both of Harford County, married 15 May
1791 (they were married by virtue of the publication of banns)

Fox, Mary and Thomas Chambers married 6 Aug 1748 (another entry in the
parish register indicated they married subsequent to 7 Jul 1748, but the exact
date was not given, and her name was listed as Cox)

Fraisher, Kezia and Thomas Brown married 13 Apr 1760 (her name was listed
as Phraisher in the parish register and in my 1987 book)

Franklin, Elizabeth and Malcom Macfee married in 1775 (the exact date of
marriage was not given, but their request to publish marriage banns was
entered in the parish register after one dated 10 Aug 1775)

Freeman, James and Margaret Butram married 28 Oct 1742 (another entry in the
parish register listed her name was Margrett Bertram and their marriage date
as 10 Oct 1742; the earlier date could have been their intention of marriage
or publication of banns)

Frissel, Nathan and Margaret Deason married 18 Apr 1751 (another entry in the parish register indicated they married in 1751, but the exact date was not given, and his name was listed as Frizell)

Frissel, Susanna and Allen McKenley married 23 Apr 1745 (their names were listed as Mackenley and Freziel in my 1987 book)

Frissell, John and Providence Dallerhide married 25 Oct 1722 (they were mistakenly listed as John Frissil and Providence Dallatude married -- Nov 1721 in another part of the parish register and in my 1987 book)

Frost, Joseph and Mary Baker married 2 Oct 1761 (his name was listed as Jos. or Jas. in my 1987 book)

Frost, William and Susannah Robertson married 21 Dec 1749 (another entry in the parish register indicated they married subsequent to 17 Dec 1749, but the exact date was not given, and her last name was listed as Roberson; Susannah was mistakenly listed as Suhannah in my 1987 book)

Fulks, Jacob and Priscilla Perkins, both of Baltimore County, married 13 Dec 1792 (no marriage license was found in Balimore or Harford County so they were apparently married by virtue of the publication of banns)

Fuller, Mordecai and Mary James married 6 May 1745 (another entry in the parish register indicated they married 28 Apr 1745; the earlier date could have been their intention of marriage or publication of banns)

Fullerton, James and Sarah Bradford, both of Harford County, married 13 Jan 1791 (the parish register indicated they were married by virtue of a license from Harford County, but no marriage license was found in Harford or Baltimore County)

Furness, John and Jane Green married 10 Feb 1744 (another entry in the parish register indicated they married 10 Feb 1745; the date should actually be written 10 Feb 1744/5)

Gadd, Absolom and Elizabeth Cullison married 19 Oct 1758 (his name was spelled Absolem in my 1987 book and this marriage appeared on page 217 of the register, but Gadd was missing from the index of my book)

Gadd, Christian, see "Margaret Gadd," q.v.

Gadd, Margaret, daughter of Thomas and Christian, born 28 Mar 1734 (her year of birth was mistakenly listed as 1731 in my 1987 book)

Gadd, Thomas and Christian Ditto married 21 Jan 1733 (another entry in the parish register indicated they married 22 Jan 1732/3)

Gafford, Aley and John Hambleton, both of Harford County, married 26 Jan 1797 (they were married by virtue of a license issued on 24 Jan 1797)

Gaine, Elizabeth and Thomas Cox married 13 Dec 1744 (another entry in the parish register indicated Jacob Cox and Elizabeth Gain married on this date)

Gallion, Mary and Ruthan Garrison, both of Harford County, married 23 Nov 1797 (they were married by virtue of a license issued on 20 Nov 1797)

Galloway, Absalom, see "Berthia Galloway," q.v.

Galloway, Aquila and Ann Barton, both of Baltimore County, married 4 Mar 1792 (their marriage date was mistakenly listed as 4 Apr 1792 in my 1987 book; they were married by virtue of a license issued on 18 Feb 1792 which listed their names as Acquila Galloway and Nancy Barton)

Galloway, Berthia, daughter of Absalom and Rebecca, born 26 Oct? 1790 (the date was listed only as 1790 in my 1987 book)

Galloway, Joseph (of Anne Arundel County) and Mrs. Susanna Paca (of Baltimore County) married 18 Oct 1722 (the Mrs. was omitted from her name in my 1987 book)

Galloway, Lytica, see "Walter Robinson," q.v.

Galloway, Rebecca, see "Berthia Galloway," q.v.

Garrison, Ruthan and Mary Gallion, both of Harford County, married 23 Nov 1797 (they were married by virtue of a license issued on 20 Nov 1797)

Garritt, Mary and James Quinley married 26 May 1761 (his name was difficult to read in the parish register and it could have been Quinley or Quinby)

Gaton (Guton, Guiton), Margrett and Samuel Foster married 26 Feb 1749 (another entry in the parish register indicated they married subsequent to 11 Feb 1750, but the exact date was not given, and her name was listed as Margaret Guiton)

Gaton, Benjamin and Elizabeth Shannom married 26 Oct 1750 (her name was mistakenly listed as Skinnoni in my 1987 book)

Gebbs, John and Hannah Palmer married 1 Jan 1751 (another entry in the parish register indicated they married in 1751, but the exact date was not given, and his name was listed as Gibbs)

George, Elizabeth and Richard Holloway married 26 Dec 1760 (his name was listed as Rd. and her name was listed as Eliz. in the parish register and in my 1987 book)

George, Sarah and John Brannian, both of Harford County, married 23 Jun 1791 (his name was listed as Branian in my 1987 book and as Brannion in the parish register; his name was listed as Brannian when the marriage license was issued on 21 Jun 1791)

Gibbs, John, see "John Gebbs," q.v.

Gibson, Sarah and James Rampley married 22 Sep 1771 (his name was listed as Rumpley in my 1987 book)

Gibson, Thomas and Katherine Demorse married 22 Dec 1761 (her name was listed as Kathrine Demorce in the parish register)

Gilbert, Parker and Martha McComas, both of Harford County, married 21 Sep 1797 (they were married by virtue of a license issued on 19 Nov 1797)

Gilbert, Ruth and James Billingsley married 16 Jun 1767 (his name was misspelled as Billinsgley in my 1987 book)

Gilbert, Sarah and John Morris married 31 Jul 1743 (another entry in the parish register indicated they married 28 Aug 1743)

Giles, Ann(e) and Thomas Johnson, both of Baltimore County, married 22 May 1794 (although her name was listed as Ann in my 1987 book, it was listed as Anne in the parish register and on the marriage license issued 22 May 1794)

Ginkins family names (references to this family were indicated in the index of my 1987 book, but they are not in said book; rather, they are in Reamy's *St. George's Parish Register, 1689-1793*; since the surname index to my book was prepared long ago by Lucy Harrison, it cannot now be determined how the discrepancy arose; thanks to M. A. Wagner of Wappingers Falls, New York for bringing this error to my attention)

Gittings, Elizabeth and Lambert Smith, both of Baltimore County, married 6 Nov 1792 (they were married by virtue of a license issued on 3 Nov 1792)

Gittings, Harriott, see "John Sterett Gittings," q.v.

Gittings, James, see "John Sterett Gittings," q.v.

Gittings, John Sterett, son of James and Harriott, born 22 May 1798, baptized 13 Nov 1799 (his date of baptism was listed as 15 Nov 1799 in my 1987 book)

Gittings, Susanna and Henry Bateman Goe, both of Baltimore County, married 16 Feb 1792 (they were married by virtue of a license issued on 7 Feb 1792 and listed her name as Susannah Gettings)

Godard, Elizabeth and John Wein or Weir married 8 Jan 1760 (his name could have been Ween, Wein or Weir in the parish register)

Godman, William, see "William Godwin," q.v.

Godsgrace, John, see "William Godsgrace" and "Rebecca Godsgrace," q.v.

Godsgrace, Rebecca, daughter of John and Rebecca, born 7 Mar 1740 (although her name was listed as Godigrace in the parish register and in my 1987 book, it was actually Godsgrace)

Godsgrace, William, son of John and Rebecca, born 9 Jan 1738 (although his name was listed as Godigrace in the parish register and in my 1987 book, it was actually Godsgrace)

Godwin, William and Delilah White, both of Harford County, married 22 Jul 1797 (although the parish register indicated their names were William Godman and Deliah White, *Harford County Marriage Licenses, 1777-1865* indicated a license was issued to Wm. Godwin and Delilah White on 15 Jul 1797)

Goe, Henry Bateman and Susanna Gittings, both of Baltimore County, married 16 Feb 1792 (they were married by virtue of a license issued on 7 Feb 1792 and listed her name as Susannah Gettings)

Golden, Peter and Elizabeth Earl married 15 Nov 1742 (his name was listed as Golding in other parts of the parish register and another entry in the parish register indicated they married 10 Oct 1742; the earlier date could have been their intention of marriage or publication of banns)

Gorsuch, Benjamin and Kerenhappuck Johnson married 17 Jul 1760 (her name was entered as Keren Happuck Johnson in the parish register and in my 1987 book)

Gorsuch, Dorcas and John Ensor married 2 Jul 1772 (her name was mistakenly listed as Gorsich in my 1987 book)

Gorsuch, Rachel and James Bosley married 18 Sep 1760 (their names were listed as James Bozley and Rachl. Gorsuch in the parish register)

Gott, Elizabeth (Betty) and John White married 29 Jan 1751 (another entry in the parish register indicated they married in 1751, but the exact date was not given)

Gott, Mary and Thomas Cutchin married 5 Dec 1743 (another entry in the parish register indicated they married 27 Nov 1743 and his name was listed as

Gudgins; the earlier date could have been their intention of marriage or publication of banns)

Gott, Richard and Ruth Bailey, both of Baltimore County, married 17 Dec 1795 (they were married by virtue of a license issued on 16 Dec 1795)

Gouldsmith, Sarah and John Toomy married 10 Nov 1768 (another entry in the parish register listed her name was Salley)

Graham, James and Mary Vine married 25 Dec 1753 (another entry in the parish register indicated they married subsequent to November, 1753, but the exact date was not given)

Graves, Catherine and George Thyler married 1 Jan 1748 (the date should actually be written 1 Jan 1748/9; another entry in the parish register indicated George Thayer and Katherine Graves married some time between November and December, 1748, but the exact date was not given; the earlier date could have been their intention of marriage or publication of banns)

Graves, James and Tabitha Reeves married 26 Jul 1764 (her name was listed as Tab. Reevs in the parish register)

Gray, Hannah and Edmond Standiford, both of Harford County, married 13 Oct 1787 (his first name was listed as Edmund in my 1987 book)

Gray, John and Blanch Cantwell married 30 Sep 1750 (her name was misspelled Blansh in my 1987 book)

Gray, Thomas and Mary Leggat married 29 May 1774 (her name was listed as Legget in my 1987 book)

Grayham, John and Mary McGawley, both of Harford County, married 31 Aug 1787 "by Rev. John Coleman and entered in the parish register of St. John's Parish" (her name was mistakenly listed as McGowley and the minister's name was mistakenly listed as William in my 1987 book)

Greaves, Elizabeth and James Cardel married 17 Feb 1760 (this marriage was mistakenly listed as February 71, 1760 in my 1987 book)

Green, Abraham and Ruth Carback married 25 Jun 1770 (her name was listed as Ruthe Curbeck in my 1987 book, yet another entry in the parish register listed their names as shown here)

Green, Ann and Thomas Wright, both of Harford County, married 17 Mar 1791 (they were married by virtue of a license issued in Harford County on 16 Mar 1791)

Green, Cassandra, see "Thomas Smithson Green" and "Mary Ann Green," q.v.

Green, Catherine and Lewis Puttee married 12 Jun 1722 (his name was listed as Lewis Poteet in *Maryland Marriages, 1634-1777*)

Green, Charles and Mary Colletson married 5 Jun 1753 (her name was mistakenly listed as Colletcon in my 1987 book)

Green, Jane and John Furness married 10 Feb 1744 (another entry in the parish register indicated they married 10 Feb 1745; the date should actually be written 10 Feb 1744/5)

Green, John and Elizabeth Barton married 25 Aug 1763 (his name was mistakenly listed as John Breen in my 1987 book)

Green, John, see "Mary Ann Green" and "Thomas Smithson Green," q.v.

Green, Joseph and Mary Bown married 25 Feb 1744 (the date should actually be written 25 Feb 1744/5; another entry in the parish register indicated Joseph Green and Mary Bowen married 24 Feb 1745)

Green, Mary and James Morgan married 12 Nov 1749 (another entry in the parish register indicated they married between 24 Sep and 26 Nov 1749, but the exact date was not given)

Green, Mary Ann, daughter of John and Cassandra, born 20 Feb 1794 (the date was mistakenly listed as 16 Jan 1793 in my 1987 book)

Green, Richard and Elizabeth Feluallen married 2 Sep 1743 (her name was listed as Flualler in *Maryland Marriages, 1634-1777* and was misspelled as Henallen in my 1987 book; another entry in the parish register indicated they married 31 Jul 1743; the earlier date could have been their intention of marriage or publication of banns)

Green, Robert and Unity Corbin married 21 Sep 1746 (another entry in the parish register indicated they married 25 Sep 1746)

Green, Temperance and Ephraim Stevens married 28 Jan 1768 (his name was listed as Eprmarried in the parish register)

Green, Thomas Smithson, son of John and Cassandra, born 3 Oct 1795 (the date was mistakenly listed as 26 Feb 1794 in my 1987 book)

Greenfield, Elizabeth, daughter of William and Elizabeth, born 25 Feb 1786 (the year was omitted from my 1987 book)

Greenfield, Elizabeth, see "Sarah Greenfield," q.v.

Greenfield, Martha and Thomas Waltham, both of Harford County, married 21 May 1795 (they were married by virtue of a license issued in Harford County on that same day and it listed her name was Patty)

Greenfield, Sarah, daughter of William and Elizabeth, born 11 Jun 1788 (the year was mistakenly listed as 1798 in my 1987 book)

Greenfield, William, see "Elizabeth Greenfield" and "Sarah Greenfield," q.v.

Greening, Samuel and Ann Twine married 1 Mar 1714 (his name was listed as Grinin in my 1987 book)

Greenway, Joseph and Elizabeth Tilley married 25 Jan 1746 (his name appeared on page 195 of the parish register, but it is missing from the index of my 1987 book)

Greer, James and Eliner Hughs married 24 Mar 1768 (this appeared as "Jas. Greer & Eliner Hughs marrd. Mar. 24, 1768" in the parish register; they were listed twice in *Maryland Marriages, 1634-1777*, once as Jos. Greer and Eliner Hughes married 24 Mar 1768 and once as James Greer and Eliner Hughes married 24 May 1768)

Greer, Mosess and Mary Bayley married "in the month of January, 1737" (this marriage was entered in the parish register among the 1753 marriages)

Griffin, John and Ann Tharp married 4 Mar 1753 (her name was listed as Harp in my 1987 book)

Griffin, Richard and Jane Loyd married 21 Dec 1749 (another entry in the parish register indicated they married some time between 26 Nov and 17 Dec 1749, but the exact date was not given, and her name was listed as Jean Lord; the earlier date could have been their intention of marriage or publication of banns)

Griffin, Sarah, see "Sarah Griffith," q.v.

Griffith, Sarah and Thomas Deadman married 2 Oct 1749 (another entry in the parish register indicated they married 24 Sep 1749 and her name was listed as Griffin; the earlier date could have been their intention of marriage or publication of banns)

Grimes, Elizabeth and Abraham Hilton, both of Baltimore County, married 20 Oct 1789 (although his name was listed as Felton in one part of the parish register and looked like Helton in another part, a marriage license was issued to Abraham Hilton on 14 Oct 1789)

Grimes, Elizabeth, see "John N. Grimes," q.v.

Grimes, John N., son of John and Elizabth, born 30 Mar 1798, baptized 20 Aug 1799 (his date of baptism was incomplete in my 1987 book)

Grimes, Sarah and George Ellender, both of Baltimore County, married 12 Feb 1792 (his name was listed as Ellinder in my 1987 book; they were married by virtue of a license from Baltimore County as noted in the parish register; the license was issued on 10 Feb 1792 and listed his name as Elender)

Grinin, Samuel, see "Samuel Greening," q.v.

Groom, Mary and John Hollis married 12 Aug 1749 (another entry in the parish register indicated they married 30 Jul 1749; the earlier date could have been their intention of marriage or publication of banns)

Grover, George Sr. and Magdelen Kelly married -- Jul 1727 (this marriage was listed twice in the parish register, once with the Sr. and once without it; her first name was misspelled once as Nagdelen in my 1987 book)

Grover, Sarah and John Sandage married 19 Sep 1751 (another entry in the parish register indicated they married 25 Aug 1751 and his name was listed as Sandige; the earlier date could have been their intention of marriage or publication of banns)

Grover, William and Anne Harrod married 23 Nov 1746 (another entry in the parish register indicated they married 2 Dec 1746 and listed her name as Ann Harwood; the earlier date could have been their intention of marriage or publication of banns)

Groves, Kitty and John Sullivan married 25 Dec 1771 (their names were listed as John Soullavin and Kitty Grooves in the parish register)

Groves, Mary, see "Sarah Groves," q.v.

Groves, Mary and Samuel Beck married 5 Dec 1753 (another entry in the parish register indicated they married in 1753, but the exact date was not given)

Groves, Sarah and John Childs married 22 Jul 1752 (the entry in the parish register indicated they married subsequent to May, 1752, but the exact date was not given and her name was listed as Mary Groves)

Grunden, Ann and Edward Daws, both of Harford County, married 29 Dec 1793 (they were married by virtue of a license issued on 27 Dec 1793)

Guishard (Gosard?), Anthony and Frances Jones married 9 Feb 1752 (another entry in the parish register indicated they married subsequent to November, 1751 and spelled his name Gosard, but the exact date was not given; his name was also listed as Guyshard, but it was most likely Guishard rather than Guyshard or Gosard)

Guiton, Margaret, see "Margret Gaton (Guton)," q.v.

Guyton, Benjamin and Amelia Scarf married 13 Dec 1753 (his name was mistakenly listed as Giyton in my 1987 book)

Guyton, Frances, see "Jesse Guyton," q.v.

Guyton, Isaac and Margarett Helhorn or Hethorn, both of Harford County, married 21 Nov 1789 (although her name was listed as Fethorn in one part of the parish register and Helhorn in another part, it was listed as Hilhorn in my 1987 book and as Hethorn in *Maryland Marriages, 1778-1800*)

Guyton, Jesse, son of John and Frances, born 18 May 1801, baptized 28 Sep 1801 (this entry was inadvertently omitted from my 1987 book)

Guyton, John, see "Jesse Guyton," q.v.

Guyton, Ruth and John Watkins, both of Baltimore County, married 2 Jun 1796 (they were married by virtue of a license issued on 31 May 1796)

Hadmington, William and Elizabeth Bosley married 23 Mar 1769 (her name was listed as Bozley in my 1987 book)

Hakman, Anne and Thomas Lomax married -- Jan 1726 (this marriage was not listed in *Maryland Marriages, 1634-1777*)

Haley, Sarah and James Smith, both of Harford County, married 20 Sep 1797 (the marriage date was mistakenly listed as 21 Sep 1797 in my 1987 book; they were issued a marriage license on 20 Sep 1797 and married the same day)

Hall, Ann and Aquila, see "Edward Carvill Hall," q.v.

Hall, Delia(h) and Philip Moore, both of Baltimore County, married 30 Apr 1799 (another entry in the parish register indicated they married on 13 Apr 1799; *Maryland Marriages, 1778-1800* indicated they married on 30 Apr 1799; no marriage license was found in Baltimore or Harford County to verify the date, so the earlier date could have been their intention of marriage or publication of banns)

Hall, Edward Carvill, son of Aquila and Ann, born 31 Nov 1797 (the date was listed as 23 Nov 1797 in my 1987 book and even though there are 30 days in November the entry in the parish register gave the date as 31 Nov 1797)

Hall, Jacob, see "Mary Hall," q.v.

Hall, Ketura(h) and Joseph Deason married 23 Nov 1746 (another entry in the parish register indicated they married 27 Nov 1746)

Hall, Mary and John Deason married 1 May 1749 (another entry in the parish register indicated they married between 26 Mar 1749 and 14 May 1749, but the exact date was not given)

Hall, Mary, daughter of Dr. Jacob and Mary, born 30 Oct 1793 (the date was mistakenly listed as 3 Oct 1793 in my 1987 book and the title of Dr. was inadvertently omitted)

Hall, Mary (daughter of Col. John Hall of Baltimore County) and Benjamin Rumsey (of Cecil County, attorney at law) married 24 Mar 1768 (the year of marriage was omitted from my 1987 book)

Hall, Samuel and Ann(e) King married 9 Feb 1746 (the date should actually be written 9 Feb 1745/6; another entry in the parish register indicated Samuel Hill and Ann King married 9 Feb 1745; *Baltimore County Families, 1659-1759* indicated his name was Samuel Hall)

Hambleton, Elizabeth and William Roach, both of Harford County, married 27 Jan 1793 (they were married by virtue of the publication of banns)

Hambleton, John and Peggy Bond, both of Harford County, married 17 Jun 1793 (they were married by virtue of a license issued that same day and listed her name as Margaretta Bond)

Hambleton, John and Aley Gafford, both of Harford County, married 26 Jan 1797 (they were married by virtue of a license issued on 24 Jan 1797)

Hammond, Eliner and James McDuggle married 28 Jun 1747 (his name was mistakenly listed as James M. Duggle in my 1987 book; *Maryland Marriages, 1634-1777* mistakenly listed his name as James M. M'Duggle)

Hance, Addam and Ruth Sutton married 25 Oct 1744 (another entry in the parish register indicated Adam Hendress and Ruth Sutton married subsequent to 23 Sep 1744, but the exact date was not given)

Handland, John and Mary Cantwell married in 1749 (the exact date was not given, but it was apparently some time in July 1749)

Hanson, Sarah and Michael Craws, both of Harford County, married 28 Feb 1788 (her name was mistakenly listed as Hauson in my 1987 book)

Hardesty, Joshua and Keziah Taylor married 5 Oct 1746 (another entry in the parish register indicated Joshua Hargisty and Kezie Taylor married 6 Oct 1746)

Harman, William and Sarah Powell married 24 Jun 1744 (another entry in the parish register indicated William Harmon and Sarah Powel married 17 Jun 1744)

Harps, Susannah and John Oggdon married 19 Nov 1748 (another entry in the parish register indicated they married 23 Oct 1748 and his name was listed as Oakdin; the earlier date could have been their intention of marriage or publication of banns)

Harrard, Mary and William Anderson married 21 Aug 1755 (her name was difficult to read in the parish register and it could have been Harrard or Haward)

Harrington, Elizabeth, born 27 Dec 1789 (although the names of her parents were missing from the parish register and noted as such in my 1987 book, she was probably the daughter of Thomas Harrington and Biddy Howard who obtained a marriage license in Baltimore County on 2 Jun 1781)

Harriott, Ann, wife of Oliver Harriott, died 13 May 1716 (their name was listed as Harrit in my 1987 book)

Harriott, Oliver and Susanna Morrow married 17 Jan 1717 (their names were listed as Oliver Harrett and Susannah Morrow in my 1987 book)

Harriott, Susannah and William Cock married 18 Jun 1752 (her name was misspelled Susanhah in my 1987 book)

Harris, James and Cassandra James married 4 Jun 1771 (her name was listed as Cassandera in the parish register)

Harris, John and Dorothy Rogers married -- Dec 1721 (the day of marriage was not indicated in the parish register and his name was mistakenly listed as James Harris in *Maryland Marriages, 1634-1777*)

Harrod, Ann(e) and William Grover married 23 Nov 1746 (another entry in the parish register indicated they married 2 Dec 1746 and listed her name as Ann Harwood; the earlier date could have been their intention of marriage or publication of banns)

Harryman, Ann and Thomas Davinn married 10 Sep 1771 (her name was mistakenly listed as Harmpmann in my 1987 book)

Harryman, Charles and Elizabeth Raven married 6 Feb 1752 (her name was listed as Reaven in the parish register)

Harryman, George and Sarah Raven married 17 Oct 1749 (her name was listed as Reaven in the parish register)

Harryman, John and Elizabeth Clark married 19 May 1752 (her name was listed as Clerk in my 1987 book)

Harryman, Tabitha and John Hughs married 23 May 1771 (her name was listed as Haryman in my 1987 book)

Hart, Henry and Mary Cartwright married 12 Dec 1780 (her name was mistakenly listed as Mart in my 1987 book)

Hartley, Ezekiel, son of Thomas and Leah, born 1792, baptized -- Sep 1793 (this entry was inadvertently omitted from my 1987 book)

Hartley, Sarah, daughter of Thomas and Leah, born 1791 (the exact date was not given; this entry was inadvertently omitted from my 1987 book)

Harwood, Ann, see "Ann Harrod," q.v.

Hatten, ---- (a reference to this name was indicated in the index of my 1987 book as being on page 323 of the parish register, but it is neither in my book nor in Reamy's *St. George's Parish Register, 1689-1793*; since the surname index to my book was prepared long ago by Lucy Harrison, it cannot now be determined how the discrepancy arose)

Hatten (Hatton), Aquila and Elizabeth Crook married 29 Dec 1767 (this marriage was inadvertently omitted from my 1987 book; thanks to Helyn Hatton Collison of Cockeysville, Maryland for bringing this omission to my attention)

Hatten, Chainey and Keziah Bayley married 31 Dec 1761 (her name was listed as Kez. in the parish register)

Hatten, Thomas and Cathrine Bayley married 29 Jan 1767 (his name was misspelled Hatlin in my 1987 book)

Hatton, John and Sarah Chieney married 17 May 1733 (his name was listed as Hatten and her surname as Chienie in my 1987 book)

Hatton, Susannah, see "Susanna Chamberlain," q.v.

Haundrix, Cathrine and Benjamin Hendrixson married 28 Apr 1763 (her name was mistakenly listed as Hanndrix in my 1987 book)

Haward, Mary, see "Mary Harrard," q.v.

Hawkins, Jos. and Sarah Macdanile married 19 May 1744 (his name was listed as Jos. or Jas. in my 1987 book and her name was probably McDaniel)

Hawkins, Robert and Avarilla Mitchell married 19 May 1772 (his name was mistakenly listed as Robert Hawlines in my 1987 book and her name was listed as Arebella Mitchel in the parish register)

Hays, Edmond and Mary Smith married -- Nov 1731 (his first name was listed as Edmond in my 1987 book and as Edmund in *Baltimore County Families, 1659-1759*, but this marriage was not listed in *Maryland Marriages, 1634-1777*)

Hays, Mary and John Norrington, John married 1 Aug 1737 (his name was listed as Norrinton in my 1987 book)

Hedington, Zebulon and Elizabeth Lemmon married 31 Mar 1771 (his name was mistakenly listed as Ribulon on my 1987 book; her name was listed as Eliz. in the parish register)

Heldebroad, Deowald and Mary Pickett married 8 Jul 1753 (although it appeared to be Heldebroad in the parish register his name could have been Hildebrand)

Helm, John and Cueler Bosley married 2 Sep 1762 (her name was listed as Bozley in the parish register)

Henderside, William and Mary Williams married 18 Aug 1771 (their request to publish marriage banns was entered in the parish register on 27 Jul 1771 and his name was subsequently listed as Handerside)

Hendon, Prudence and Sutton Sickelmore married 29 Jul 1762 (their names were listed as Sicklemore and Hindon in my 1987 book)

Hendrixson, Benjamin and Cathrine Haundrix married 28 Apr 1763 (her name was mistakenly listed as Hanndrix in my 1987 book)

Henly, Edward, see "James Henly," q.v.

Henly, James, son of Edward and Mary, born 3 Dec 1716 (although his first name was listed as Jeames and his date of birth was listed as 3 -- 1716 in my 1987 book, he was listed as James Henly, born 3 Dec 1716 in *Baltimore County Families, 1659-1759*)

Henly, Mary, see "James Henly," q.v.

Henly, Mary and Henry James married 26 Jun 1745 (her name was misspelled Hernly in my 1987 book and was listed as Henley in *Maryland Marriages, 1634-1777*)

Henly, Rachel and Greenberry Debrular married 23 May 1799 (they were married by virtue of a license issued that same day; her name was misspelled Healey and listed as Henley in other parts of the parish register)

Herrington, Hannah, daughter of Jacob and Hannah, born 31 Mar 1723 (although her date of birth was listed as 31 Mar 17-- in my 1987 book, it was noted as 31 Mar 1723 in *Baltimore County Families, 1659-1759*)

Herrington, Jacob, see "Hannah Herrington," q.v.

Herrington, Katherine and Samuel Sickelmore married 12 Sep 1716 (their names were listed as Samevall Scickemore and Katerne Herrington in the parish register and in my 1987 book)

Hethorn (Helhorn), Margarett and Isaac Guyton, both of Harford County, married 21 Nov 1789 (although her name was listed as Fethorn in one part of the parish register and Helhorn in another part, it was listed as Hilhorn in my 1987 book and as Hethorn in *Maryland Marriages, 1778-1800*)

Hickerson, Samuel (of Baltimore County) and Mary Thrap (of Harford County) married 13 Nov 1788 (her name was mistakenly listed as Throp in my 1987 book)

Hicks, Tabitha and Richard Cross married 1 Jan 1761 (her name was listed as Tab. Hixs in the parish register and in my 1987 book)

Hicks, William and Tabitha Stansbury married 24 Dec 1747 (another entry in the parish register indicated they married some time between 6 Dec 1747 and 3 Jan 1748, but the exact date was not given)

Hickson (Hixson), Ann(e) and John Crockett married 25 Dec 1744 (another entry in the parish register indicated John Crokat and Anne Hixson married on this date while another entry misspelled her name as Fixson)

Higgins, Anne and John Peacocke married -- May 1747 (the entry in the parish register indicated they married some time between 10 May and 17 May 1747, but the exact date was not given)

Hildebrand, Deowald, see "Deowald Heldebroad," q.v.

Hildebrand, Mary and William Pollard married 19 May 1755 (her name was difficult to read in the parish register and it could have been Hildebrand or Heldebroad)

Hill, Elizabeth and William Pollet married in 1753 (the complete date was not given in the parish register)

Hill, Frances and Christopher Dives married 10 Dec 1728 (his name was listed as Divas in the parish register and also in my 1987 book, but the more common spellings of the name were Dives or Divers; it was mistakenly listed as Davis in *Maryland Marriages, 1634-1777*)

Hill, Martha and Henry Dawney married 12 Sep 1799 (they were married by virtue of a license issued on 10 Sep 1799)

Hill, Mary and James Cosley married 3 Jan 1744 (another entry in the parish register indicated they married some time between 25 Dec 1744 and 28 Jan 1745, but the exact date was not given; his name was also listed as Costley)

Hill, Samuel, see "Samuel Hall," q.v.

Hillen, Alexander and Susanna Durham married 16 May 1799 (they were married by virtue of a license issued that same day; his name was listed as Hellen in another part of the parish register)

Hillen, Elizabeth and James McComas married 15 Nov 1761 (his name was entered as Jas. Maccomas in the parish register and her name was listed as Eliz. Hillin)

Hilton, Abraham and Elizabeth Grimes, both of Baltimore County, married 20 Oct 1789 (although his name was listed as Felton in one part of the parish register and looked like Helton in another part, a marriage license was issued to Abraham Hilton on 14 Oct 1789)

Hilton, Abraham, see "Patty Hilton" and "Betsey Hilton," q.v.

Hilton, Betsey, daughter of Abraham and Elizabeth, born 18 Jun 1795 (this entry was inadvertently omitted from my 1987 book)

Hilton, Elizabeth, see "Patty Hilton" and "Betsey Hilton," q.v.

Hilton, John, see "Keturah Hilton," q.v.

Hilton, Keturah, daughter of John and Lydia, born 27 Dec 1797, baptized 10 Mar 1798 (her date of baptism was omitted from my 1987 book)

Hilton, Lydia, see "Keturah Hilton," q.v.

Hilton, Patty, daughter of Abraham and Elizabeth, born 12 Jan 1793 (her date of birth was listed as 13 Jan 1793 in my 1987 book)

Hindon (Hendon), Joss. or Josh. and Hannah Starkey married 9 Jan 1766 (his name was difficult to read in the parish register, but it could be Joss. with an elevated "s" or Josh. with an elevated "h" and his last name was either Hindon or Hendon)

Hines, Mary and Mordecai Kelly married 6 Jan 1757 (his name was listed as Mordicai Kelley in my 1987 book; *Maryland Marriages, 1634-1777* mistakenly listed their marriage date as 19 Nov 1757, but that was the date of birth for their first child John)

Hipkins, Charles and Elizabeth Myers, both of Baltimore County, married 10 May 1789 (her name was listed as Mires in my 1987 book, but it was listed as Myers and Myres in different parts of the parish register)

Hitchcock, Anne and Peter Carroll married 8 Jun 1739 (his name was listed as Carrall in my 1987 book)

Hitchcock, Asael and Sarah Norris married 8 Oct 1742 (another entry in the parish register indicated they married 8 Oct 1741)

Hitchcock, Elizabeth and Seaborn Tucker married 9 Nov 1762 (his name was mistakenly listed as Tuckin in my 1987 book)

Hitchcock, Emelie and Peter Whitaker married 12 Feb 1744 (another entry in the parish register indicated they married 10 Feb 1745 and her name was listed as Amelia; the date should actually be written 12 Feb 1744/5)

Hitchcock, Jemima and Sabret Tayman married 16 Jan 1742/3 (his name was misspelled Tayrman in my 1987 book)

Hitchcock, Jemima and Piercey Potett married 12 Oct 1743 (his name was listed as Potelt in *Maryland Marriages, 1634-1777*)

Hobeard, Thomas and Dinah Morel married 3 Mar 1771 (her name was listed as Marel in my 1987 book)

Hodge, Philip and Jane Sutton married 13 Mar 1774 (her name was listed as Sutten in my 1987 book)

Holland, Francis and Sybell West, both of Baltimore County, married 25 May 1797 (they were married by virtue of a license issued on 18 May 1797)

Holland, Sarah and John McCubbin married 29 Jan 1761 (his name was listed as Jno. M'Cubbin in the parish register)

Holland, Thomas and Ann Vitean married 12 Dec 1766 (her last name could have been spelled either Vitean or Viteau in the parish register)

Hollis, John and Mary Groom married 12 Aug 1749 (another entry in the parish register indicated they married 30 Jul 1749; the earlier date could have been their intention of marriage or publication of banns)

Holloway, Richard and Elizabeth George married 26 Dec 1760 (his name was listed as Rd. and her name was listed as Eliz. in the parish register and in my 1987 book)

Holt, Arnold and Martha Boarding married 11 Feb 1744 (another entry in the parish register indicated they married 10 Feb 1745; the date should actually be written 11 Feb 1744/5)

Hooper, Frances and Thomas Watson married 24 Mar 1761 (her name was listed as Fra. in the parish register and his name was spelled Wattson in my 1987 book)

Hooper, John and Sarah Jernes or Jerves married 19 Sep 1765 (her last name was difficult to read in the parish register, but it could be Jernes or Jerves)

Hope, James and Eliner Demorse married 24 May 1768 (her name was listed as Demorce in the parish register)

Hopkins, Charles (of Harford County) and Nancy or Ann Jenkins (of Baltimore County) married 23 Jul 1793 (although her name was listed as Ann and Anna in the parish register, it was listed as Nancy on the marriage license issued in Harford County on 22 Jul 1793)

Horner, Nathan and Delia Carroll, both of Harford County, married 2 May 1799 (another entry in the parish register mistakenly listed his name as Former; they were married by virtue of a license issued on 30 Apr 1799 and listed his name as Horner)

Horner, Sarah and John York married 16 Oct 1752 (the year was clearly written as 1752 in the parish register, but the information was entered among the October, 1751 marriages)

Horton, Mary and John White married in 1749 (the exact date was not given in the parish register, but apparently they married some time between 26 Mar and 14 May 1749)

House, John, see "John Hows," q.v.

Householder, Henry and Mary Jonas married 16 Feb 1769 (his name was listed as Hen. in the parish register)

Howard, Ann and Charles Lin married 26 May 1768 (his name was listed as Cha. in the parish register)

Howard, Biddy, see "Elizabeth Harrington," q.v.

Howard, Edward Aquila (of Baltimore) and Charlotte Rumsey (of Harford County) married 11 Dec 1798 (they were married by virtue of a license issued on 10 Dec 1798)

Howard, Elizabeth and Thomas Sadler, both of Baltimore County, married 7 Nov 1793 (they were married by virtue of a license issued on 6 Nov 1793 and it listed her name as Eliza G. Howard)

Howard, Frances Cordelia, daughter of Thomas Gassaway Howard and ----, born 13 Nov 1795 (the date was listed as 18 Nov 1795 in my 1987 book and his middle name was misspelled Gassoway)

Howard, Sarah and James McComas, both of Harford County, married 29 May 1794 (the marriage date was mistakenly listed as 29 Mar 1794 in my 1987 book; their marriage license was issued 27 May 1794)

Howard, Susanna and James Walter Tolley married 21 May 1799 (they were married by virtue of a license issued on 18 May 1799)

Howard, Thomas Gassaway and Martha Susanna Tolley, both of Baltimore County, married 2 Apr 1793 (they were married by virtue of a license issued on 1 Apr 1793 and listed her name as Martha Tolly; it should also be noted that *Baltimore County Marriage Licenses, 1777-1798* mistakenly listed her name was Tally)

Howard, Thomas Gassaway, see "Frances Cordelia Howard," q.v.

Howlet, Robert and Elizabeth Boone married in 1771 (the exact date of marriage was not given, but their request to publish marriage banns was entered in the parish register some time between 27 Jul 1771 and 15 Sep 1771)

Hows, John and Penelepy Bond married 22 Jul 1750 (another entry in the parish register indicated John House and Penclope Bond married some time between February and August, 1750, but the exact date was not given)

Hudson, William and Sarah Deason married 30 Jan 1749 (the date should actually be 30 Jan 1749/50; another entry in the parish register indicated they married subsequent to 17 Dec 1749, but the exact date was not given)

Huggins, Ann(e) and William Jones married 2 May 1745 (another entry in the parish register indicated they married 14 Apr 1745; the earlier date could have been their intention of marriage or publication of banns)

Huggins, John Jr. and Mary Downs married 7 Oct 1742 (another entry in the parish register indicated John Hugins and Mary Downes married 29 Aug 1742; the earlier date could have been their intention of marriage or publication of banns)

Hughes, Rachel and Jonas Stevenson married 12 May 1799 (they were married by virtue of a license issued on 10 May 1799)

Hughes, William and Ann Bellows married 24 Jun 1743 (his name was listed as Hughs in my 1987 book)

Hughs, Eliner and James Greer married 24 Mar 1768 (this appeared as "Jas. Greer & Eliner Hughs marrd. Mar. 24, 1768" in the parish register; they were listed twice in *Maryland Marriages, 1634-1777*, once as Jos. Greer and Eliner Hughes married 24 Mar 1768 and once as James Greer and Eliner Hughes married 24 May 1768)

Hughs, John and Tabitha Harryman married 23 May 1771 (her name was listed as Haryman in my 1987 book)

Hughson, Rebecca and Mosess Campbell married "in the month of June, 1751" (this marriage was entered in the parish register among the 1758 marriages)

Hunter, Nancy and Benjamin Parish, both of Baltimore County, married 1 Mar 1792 (they were married by virtue of a license issued on 18 Feb 1792)

Husband, Lucia and Zacharias Durham, both of Harford County, married 11 Mar 1792 (they were married by virtue of the publication of banns)

Hutchens, Richard and Phillisanna Standiford married 20 Jan 1767 (her name was listed as Philliszaner Standeford in the parish register)

Hutchens, Thomas and Hannah Seemons married 12 May 1736 (her name was misspelled Seemmons in my 1987 book)

Hutchenson, Simon and Pennil Brooker married 12 Aug 1750 (another entry in the parish register indicated Simon Hutchison and Penelope Brooke married in August 1750, but the day was not given)

Hutcheson, Simon and Anne Newman married 24 Aug 1746 (another entry in the parish register indicated Simon Hutchinson and Ann Newman married 25 Aug 1746)

Hutchins, Nicholas Jr. and Mary Standiford married 4 Jan 1763 (her name was listed as Standeford in my 1987 book)

Ingram, Susanna, daughter of Leven and Hannah, born 1 Nov 1770 (her name was misspelled Susanhah in my 1987 book)

Ingrim, Mary and Ashell Roberts married 16 Dec 1742 (his name was misspelled Asraell in my 1987 book; another entry in the parish register indicated Asahell Roberts and Mary Ingram married 5 Dec 1742; the earlier date could have been their intention of marriage or publication of banns)

Inman (Lumon?), Ann and Williams Pinkstone married -- Oct 1743 (her name was listed as Lumon in *Maryland Marriages, 1634-1777*)

Isham (Ishum), James and Elizabeth Robinson married ---- (no date was given in the parish register, but it was listed among the 1717-1718 marriages; his name was mistakenly listed as Jeames Isinn (Lsinn) in my 1987 book; James Isham or Ishum married Elizabeth Robinson, admx. of William Robinson, by June 1719, as noted in *Baltimore County Families, 1659-1759*)

Israel, Esther and Andrew McClean married 2 Dec 1800 (another entry in the parish register indicated Andrew McCleary and Esther Israel were married on 1 Dec 1800)

Jackman, Elizabeth and John Everett married 5 May 1771 (their names were listed as John Everat and Eliz. Jackman in the parish register)

Jackson, Ellinor (widow) and John O'Bryan married 24 Sep 1721 (they were listed as John Bryan and Elinor Jackson in *Maryland Marriages, 1634-1777*)

Jackson, Mary and William Kimber married 19 Aug 1749 (another entry in the parish register indicated they married some time between 30 Jul and 20 Aug 1749, but the exact date was not given; his name was mistakenly listed as Kimler or Krinler in my 1987 book)

Jacobs, John and Mary Lynch married 29 Mar 1761 (his name was listed as John Jacob in my 1987 book)

James, Cassandra and James Harris married 4 Jun 1771 (her name was listed as Cassandera in the parish register)

James, Eliakim, see "William James," q.v.

James, Elizabeth and Ickett Jones married 14 Dec 1746 (another entry in the parish register indicated they married 16 Dec 1746)

James, Frances and Thomas Nichols married 21 Aug 1740 (this marriage was entered in the parish register among the 1744 marriages)

James, Henry and Mary Henly married 26 Jun 1745 (her name was misspelled Hernly in my 1987 book and was listed as Henley in *Maryland Marriages, 1634-1777*)

James, John and Avarilla Standiford married 14 Apr 1761 (her name was listed as Standeford in my 1987 book)

James, Margaret and Joseph Wright married in 1750 (the complete date was not given in the parish register)

James, Mary and Mordecai Fuller married 6 May 1745 (another entry in the parish register indicated they married 28 Apr 1745; the earlier date could have been their intention of marriage or publication of banns)

James, Mary and James Auger married 1 Jan 1756 (his name was misspelled Anger in my 1987 book)

James, Parmela, see "William James," q.v.

James, Walter and Cordelia Legoe married 23 Dec 1762 (his name was listed as Walt. James in the parish register)

James, William, son of Eliakim and Parmela, born 6 Oct 1798, baptized 14 May 1799 (his parents' names were mistakenly listed as Eliakins and Pamela in my 1987 book)

Jane (Jasie?), Mary and William Fleming married 5 Nov 1759 (her last name was difficult to read in the parish register, but it could have been Jane or Jasie)

Jarvis, John and Sarah Wright married 2 Jul 1761 (his name was listed as Jno. Jarves in the parish register)

Jeffreys, John and Sarah Williams married 14 Nov 1749 (his name was misspelled Jeffriys in my 1987 book; another entry in the parish register indicated they married 28 May 1749 and his name was listed as Jeffrey; the earlier date could have been their intention of marriage or publication of banns)

Jenkins, Andrew and Elizabeth Boyd married 12 Jan 1743 (the date should actually be written 12 Jan 1743/4; another entry in the parish register indicated Henry Jenkins and Elizabeth Boyd married 25 Dec 1743; the earlier date could have been their intention of marriage or publication of banns)

Jenkins, Ann (of Baltimore County) and Charles Hopkins (of Harford County) married 23 Jul 1793 (although her name was listed as Ann and Anna in the parish register, it was listed as Nancy on the marriage license issued in Harford County on 22 Jul 1793)

Jenkins, Henry, see "Andrew Boyd," q.v.

Jennings, Joseph and Mary Rider married 23 May 1743 (his name was mistakenly listed as Lennings and Jenings in my 1987 book and the year of marriage was mistakenly listed as 1742; another entry in the parish register indicated they married 24 Apr 1743; the earlier date could have been their intention of marriage or publication of banns)

Jennings, Mary and John Boswell married 17 Nov 1745 (another entry in the parish register listed their names as Bozwell and Jenings)

Jennings, William and Hannah Rutledge married 20 Aug 1770 (her name was listed as Rutlidge in my 1987 book)

Jephs, Elizabeth and John Boyce married 30 Nov 1721 (his name was listed as Boice in my 1987 book and her name, although unusual, was listed as shown here)

Jerman, Benjamin and Elizabeth Rutledge married 28 Nov 1753 (another entry in the parish register indicated they married in 1753, but the exact date was not given; his name was listed as Terman or Jerman in my 1987 book)

Jernes (Jerves?), Sarah and John Hooper married 19 Sep 1765 (her last name was difficult to read in the parish register, but it could be Jernes or Jerves)

Johnson, Ann and Charles Kinzel (Kinzell), both of Harford County, married 8 Feb 1798 (they were married by virtue of a license issued that same day and listed his name as Kinzil)

Johnson, Israel, son of Thomas and Mary, born 20 Dec 1722 (the year of birth was omitted from my 1987 book)

Johnson, Karran and William Elliott married 17 May 1740 (this marriage was entered in the parish register among the 1752 marriages)

Johnson, Kerenhappuck and Benjamin Gorsuch married 17 Jul 1760 (her name was entered as Keren Happuck Johnson in the parish register and in my 1987 book)

Johnson, Margrett and Thomas Littlejohn married 19 Nov 1751 (his name was entered in the parish register as Thomas Little John)

Johnson, Mary, see "Israel Johnson," q.v.

Johnson, Rachel, see "Joshua Johnson Whitaker," q.v.

Johnson, Tabitha and Daniel McComas Jr. married 26 Jan 1743 (his name was listed as Maccomas in the parish register)

Johnson, Thomas and Ann(e) Giles, both of Baltimore County, married 22 May 1794 (although her name was listed as Ann in my 1987 book, it was listed as Anne in the parish register and on the marriage license issued 22 May 1794)

Johnson, Thomas and Elizabeth Taylor, both of Harford County, married 17 Nov 1796 (they were married by virtue of a license issued on 12 Nov 1796)

Johnson, Thomas (of Harford County) and Elizabeth Cord (of Baltimore County) married 17 Jun 1792 (they were married by virtue of a license issued in Baltimore County on 15 Jun 1792; his name was listed as Johnston in another part of the parish register, but it was listed as Johnson on the marriage license)

Johnson, Thomas, see "Israel Johnson," q.v.

Jonas, Mary and Henry Householder married 16 Feb 1769 (his name was listed as Hen. in the parish register)

Jones, Ann and Peter Delevit, both of Baltimore County, married 16 Feb 1794 (his name was listed as Delivett in my 1987 book, but it was also listed as Delevit in the parish register and as Delevet when the marriage license was issued on 12 Feb 1794)

Jones, Charles and Hannah Nichols married 26 Dec 1752 (another entry in the parish register indicated they married in 1752, but the exact date was not given, and her name was listed as Nicholes)

Jones, Deborah and John Row married 17 Dec 1761 (her name was listed as Deb. in the parish register)

Jones, Emanuel and Martha Parkew married 14 Aug 1757 (her name could have been spelled Parkew or Parken in the parish register)

Jones, Frances and Anthony Gosard married 9 Feb 1752 (another entry in the parish register indicated they married subsequent to November, 1751, but the exact date was not given; his name was listed as Guyshard, but it was most likely Guishard rather than Guyshard or Gosard)

Jones, John and Sarah Poulson married 14 Jul 1748 (another entry in the parish register indicated they married subsequent to 7 Jul 1748, but the exact date was not given; the marriage date was mistakenly listed as 14 Jul 1749 in my 1987 book)

Jones, John and Sarah Morris married 28 Mar 1749 (another entry in the parish register indicated "John Jones and Sarah Morris this court married" subsequent to 26 Mar 1749, but the exact date was not given)

Jones, Magdaline (of Harford County) and Martin Renshaw (of Baltimore County) married 19 Nov 1788 (her first name was listed as Madgalen in my 1987 book)

Jones, Morgan and Cordelia Baker, both of Harford County, married 25 Jan 1798 (the parish register indicated they were married by virtue of a license issued on 24 Jan 1798; *Harford County Marriage Licenses, 1777-1865* indicated the license was issued on 25 Jan 1798 and her first name was not listed on it)

Jones, Pickett and Elizabeth James married 14 Dec 1746 (another entry in the parish register indicated they married 16 Dec 1746)

Jones, Sarah and John Norton, both of Harford County, married 20 Sep 1789 (their marriage date was mistakenly listed as 24 Sep 1789 in my 1987 book)

Jones, William and Ann(e) Huggins married 2 May 1745 (another entry in the parish register indicated they married 14 Apr 1745; the earlier date could have been their intention of marriage or publication of banns)

Jones, William and Cathrine Brokley or Bochley married 23 Dec 1744 (another entry in the parish register indicated they married on this date, but listed her name as Katharine Bochley or Bechley)

Judy (Judah), Rebecca and John Mercer married 28 Feb 1765 (another entry in the parish register indicated that Rev. Hugh Deans, Rector of St. John's Parish in Baltimore County, was authorized on 18 Feb 1765 by the Honorable Horatio Sharpe, Governor of Maryland, to solemnize the marriage of John Marcer and Rebecca Judah according to law)

Juel, Magdalen and Francis Carty, both of Harford County, married 1 Oct 1792 (they were married by virtue of the publication of banns)

Keen (Cane), Elizabeth and John Warren married 16 Feb 1751 (another entry in the parish register indicated they married in 1751, but the exact date was not given)

Keen, William and Sushannah Copperwhite married 21 Nov 1757 (her last name was difficult to read in the parish register and it could have been Copperwhite or Crosswhite; her first name was listed as Sushannah in the parish register, but was misspelled as Sishannah in my 1987 book)

Keith, David and Sarah Kitely married 12 Jan 1743 (the date should actually be written 12 Jan 1743/4; another entry in the parish register indicated they married 25 Dec 1743; the earlier date could have been their intention of marriage or publication of banns)

Kelly, Isaac and Drusilla Durbin Nichols married 2 Apr 1801 (their names were listed as Kelley and Nicolls in another part of the parish register)

Kelly, John, see "Mordecai Kelly," q.v.

Kelly, Magdelen and George Grover, Sr. married -- Jul 1727 (this marriage was listed twice in the parish register, once with the Sr. and once without it; her first name was misspelled once as Nagdelen in my 1987 book)

Kelly, Mordecai and Mary Hines married 6 Jan 1757 (his name was listed as Mordicai Kelley in my 1987 book; *Maryland Marriages, 1634-1777* mistakenly listed their marriage date as 19 Nov 1757, but that was the date of birth for their first child John)

Kelsey, Ann(e) and John Trevis married 6 Dec 1743 (another entry in the parish register indicated John Travis and Anne Kelsey married 27 Nov 1743; the earlier date could have been their intention of marriage or publication of banns)

Kenhan, Coleworth and Mary Tridge married 7 Jul 1744 (his name was listed as Kenhan or Kerrhan in my 1987 book)

Kerman, Nancy, see "Nancy McCairman," q.v.

Kersey, Elizabeth and Thomas Shannom married 26 Sep 1750 (his name was listed as Shannern in my 1987 book and as Shannem in *Maryland Marriages, 1634-1777*)

Kersey, Henry, see "Henry Carey," q.v.

Kersey, John Jr. and Susannah Shaw married 27 Feb 1749 (the date should actually be written 27 Feb 1749/50; her name was mistakenly listed as Suhannah in my 1987 book)

Key, Charity and James Wear, both of Harford County, married 11 Sep 1791 (they were married by virtue of the publication of banns)

Kimber, William and Mary Jackson married 19 Aug 1749 (another entry in the parish register indicated they married some time between 30 Jul and 20 Aug 1749, but the exact date was not given; his name was mistakenly listed as Kimler or Krinler in my 1987 book)

Kimboley, Bond James and Mary Mills, both of Harford County, married 11 Sep 1787 (his name was mistakenly listed as Kimbley in my 1987 book)

King, Ann(e) and Samuel Hall married 9 Feb 1746 (the date should actually be written 9 Feb 1745/6; another entry in the parish register indicated Samuel Hill and Ann King married 9 Feb 1745; *Baltimore County Families, 1659-1759* indicated his name was Samuel Hall)

King, Deborah and Thomas McCloughon married 10 Jul 1761 (his name was listed as Thos. M'Cloughon and her first name was listed as Deb. in the parish register)

Kingstone, John and Cathrine Cheshere married 29 Apr 1754 (this marriage was inadvertently omitted from my 1987 book)

Kinnerly, Mary and James Brooks married 13 Feb 1774 (her name was listed as Kinnedy in my 1987 book)

Kinzel (Kinzell), Charles and Ann Johnson, both of Harford County, married 8 Feb 1798 (they were married by virtue of a license issued that same day and listed his name as Kinzil)

Kitely, Francis and Mary or Martha Thomas married 12 May 1751 (another entry in the parish register listed her name as Martha Thomas and indicated they married in 1751, but the exact date was not given)

Kitely, Margret and James Roose married 22 Mar 1773 (her name was mistakenly listed as Hitely in my 1987 book)

Kitely, Sarah and David Keith married 12 Jan 1743 (the date should actually be written 12 Jan 1743/4; another entry in the parish register indicated they married 25 Dec 1743 and spelled her name Kiteley; the earlier date could have been their intention of marriage or publication of banns)

Knight, Thomas and ---- Burns married 18 Jul 1763 (her first name was not recorded in the parish register)

Lacey, Susanna and Daniel O'Neall married 12 Jun 1743 (their names were listed as Daniel Oneall and Sunsannah Lacy in my 1987 book)

Lair, Joseph and Mary Bishop married 7 Jan 1742 (the date should actually be written 7 Jan 1742/3; another entry in the parish register indicated they married 19 Dec 1742 and his name was listed as Lare; the earlier date could have been their intention of marriage or publication of banns)

Lane, John and Rebecca Dorsey married 6 -- 1768 (probably married 6 Oct 1768, but the information was incomplete in the parish register)

Langden, Arthur and Mary Lewis, both of Harford County, married 25 Jan 1792 (the parish register indicated they were married by virtue of a license issued in Baltimore County, but no marriage license was found in Baltimore or Harford County; his name was listed as Longdan in another part of the parish register)

Law, John, see "John Low," q.v.

Lawrence, John and Rebecca Yarley, both of Baltimore County, married 5 Jul 1795 (they were married by virtue of the publication of banns)

Lawson, Elizabeth and John Low married 14 Nov 1758 (his name was mistakenly listed as John Law in my 1987 book)

Leech, Ambrose and Elizabeth Nairn married 7 Jul 1748 (another entry in the parish register listed their names as Ambross Leach and Elizabeth Nearn and their marriage date was mistakenly indicated as 5 Jul 1749 in my 1987 book)

Leadley, Isaac and Nancy McCubbins, both of Baltimore County, married 26 Dec 1793 (they were married by virtue of a "licence from Balt. County" as noted in the parish register, but no marriage license was found in Baltimore or Harford County; her name was listed as Mackubbins in another part the parish register)

Lecester, Nancy and Daniel Weeks married 10 Sep 1771 (his name was listed as Wheeks in the parish register and her name was listed as Lueester in my 1987 book)

Lee, Corbin S. and Mrs. Eleanor Thornton married 31 Jan 1754 (his name in my 1987 book did not include his middle initial)

Lee, Hannah and Joseph Ward married 24 Aug 1743 (another entry in the parish register indicated they married 7 Aug 1743 and his name was listed as Jr.; the earlier date could have been their intention of marriage or publication of banns)

Leekings, Mary and Ulick Burk married 14 May 1732 (his name was mistakenly listed as Buck in my 1987 book)

Legatt, Constant and Joseph Burton married 13 -- 1768 (probably married 13 Oct 1768, but the information was incomplete in the parish register)

Legatt, Joshua and Elizabeth Burk married 6 May 1766 (his name was listed as Jos. Legatt in one part of the parish register, yet there was a subsequent entry among the 1771 requests for publication of marriage banns that listed Joshua Legett and Elizabeth Burk, but the exact date was not given)

Leggatt, Mary and Thomas Gray married 29 May 1774 (her name was listed as Legget in my 1987 book)

Leggatt, William and Ann Blackett or Brackett married 13 Jul 1750 (another entry in the parish register indicated William Legat and Martha Bracket married some time between February and August, 1750, but the exact date was not given)

Legoe, Benjamin and Jean Taylor (widow) married 11 Dec 1723 (their marriage was listed as 4 Nov or 11 Dec 1723 in *Maryland Marriages, 1634-1777*; the earlier date could have been their intention of marriage or publication of banns)

Legoe, Benjamin Jr. and Judea Bruceton married 25 Oct 1740 (her name was listed as Judea Briceton or Buceton in my 1987 book and as Judeax Bruceton in *Maryland Marriages, 1634-1777*)

Legoe, Cordelia and Walter James married 23 Dec 1762 (his name was listed as Walt. James in the parish register)

Legoe, Mary and William Whealand married 21 Apr 1752 (another entry in the parish register indicated they married subsequent to November, 1751, but the exact date was not given, and his name was listed as Whaland)

Legoe, Sarah and John White married 4 Oct 1744 (another entry in the parish register indicated they married 23 Sep 1744; the earlier date could have been their intention of marriage or publication of banns)

Leitch, Sarah and John Addison, both of Baltimore County, married 11 Oct 1792 (they were married by virtue of a license issued on 5 Oct 1792 which listed her name as Sally Leech; his name was listed as John Addison, Jr. in another part of the parish register)

Lemmon, Alexius and Rachel Stansbury married 29 Nov 1771 (his name was strangely listed as Eliz'th Leemon in the parish register)

Lemmon, Elizabeth and Zebulon Hedington married 31 Mar 1771 (his name was mistakenly listed as Ribulon on my 1987 book; her name was listed as Eliz. in the parish register)

Lemmon, Mary and U. Burke married 8 Nov 1764 (his name was mistakenly listed as W. Burke in my 1987 book and he was probably Ulick Burke, born 1740, son of Thomas Burke and grandson of Ulick Burke)

Lerman, Ann and Robert Nairne married 29 Oct 1724 (her name was listed as Larman in my 1987 book)

Leshordie, Frances and Brian Cartee married 2 Jan 1750 (this marriage was entered in the parish register among the January, 1751 marriages; the date should actually be written 2 Jan 1750/1)

Lewis, Mary and Arthur Langden, both of Harford County, married 25 Jan 1792 (the parish register indicated they were married by virtue of a license issued

in Baltimore County, but no marriage license was found in Baltimore or
Harford County; his name was listed as Longdan in another part of the parish
register)

Lin, Charles and Ann Howard married 26 May 1768 (his name was listed as
Cha. in the parish register)

Linam, William and Sarah Pinix, both of Harford County, married 17 Dec 1797
(her name was listed as Pinox in my 1987 book; they were married by virtue
of a license issued on 5 Dec 1797 and listed her name as Pinix)

Linsey, Mary and Edward Felin married in 1748 (the exact date of marriage was
not given, but the entry in the parish register indicated they married
subsequent to 31 Jan 1748; *Maryland Marriages, 1634-1777* listed the
marriage as "Edward Flin and Mary Linsey, 1748")

Linzey, Mary and Richard Ellwood married 9 Oct 1748 (another entry in the
parish register listed her name as Lindsay; she was mistakenly listed as
Sinzey in my 1987 book)

Little, John and Elizabeth Adams, both of Harford County, married 20 Jul 1794
(they were married by virtue of the publication of banns)

Littlejohn, Thomas and Margrett Johnson married 19 Nov 1751 (his name was
entered in the parish register as Thomas Little John)

Lockerd, Ann and Mark Swift married 26 Dec 1725 (although her name was
misspelled Lockeord and the date of marriage was listed as 2- Dec 1725 in
my 1987 book, it was noted as Lockerd and dated 26 Dec 1725 in *Maryland
Marriages, 1634-1777*)

Lomax, Thomas and Anne Hakman married -- Jan 1726 (this marriage was not
listed in *Maryland Marriages, 1634-1777*)

Long, Martha and John Norris married 12 Nov 1772 (her name was mistakenly
listed as Marth in my 1987 book)

Long, Moses and Ann Brown married 13 Sep 1764 (his name was listed as Mos.
Long in the parish register)

Long, Peter and Margarett Carr, both of Harford County, married 30 Aug 1791
(the parish register indicated they were married by virtue of a license from
Harford County, but no marriage license was found in Harford or Baltimore
County)

Longdan, Arthur, see "Arthur Langden," q.v.

Longman, John, son of Mary, born 21 Feb 1728 (her name was mistakenly listed
as Mary Long in my 1987 book)

Lony, Benjamin and Ann Norris married 7 May 1745 (his name was mistakenly
listed as Long in my 1987 book)

Lord, Jean, see "Jane Loyd," q.v.

Lorden, George, son of George and Dinah, born 12 Apr 1727 (although listed as
such in my 1987 book, the name Lorden was not found in the index to the
parish register nor was he listed in *Maryland Marriages, 1634-1777*)

Low, Isaac and Sarah Mitchell married 5 Nov 1761 (his name was listed as
Lowe in my 1987 book)

Low, John and Susannah Cox married 29 Mar 1744 (another entry in the parish
register indicated they married 26 Mar 1744)

Low, John and Elizabeth Lawson married 14 Nov 1758 (his name was mistakenly listed as John Law in my 1987 book)

Low, Mary and Cornelius Stewart married 25 Nov 1747 (his first name was misspelled Cornelias in my 1987 book; another entry in the parish register indicated Cornelius Steward and Mary Lowe married in 1747, but the exact date was not given)

Low, Rebecca and William Perdue married 4 Feb 1747 (the date should actually be written 4 Feb 1747/8; another entry in the parish register spelled her name Lowe and indicated they married subsequent to 31 Jan 1748, but the exact date was not given)

Low, Sarah and Andrew Vaunce married 4 Jan 1745 (his name was listed as Vannce in my 1987 book)

Low, Thomas and Sarah Mainer married -- Jan 1754 (another entry in the parish register indicated they married subsequent to November, 1753, but the exact date was not given; the earlier date could have been their intention of marriage or publication of banns)

Loyd, Jane and Richard Griffin married 21 Dec 1749 (another entry in the parish register indicated they married some time between 26 Nov and 17 Dec 1749, but the exact date was not given, and her name was listed as Jean Lord; the earlier date could have been their intention of marriage or publication of banns)

Lucas, John and Sarah Divers, both of Baltimore County, married 7 Feb 1793 (her name was listed as Divins in *Maryland Marriages, 1778-1800* and as Divies in another part of the parish register; her name was listed as Divers in my 1987 book and also on their marriage license issued on 22 Jan 1793)

Lumon, Ann, see "Ann Inman," q.v.

Lusby, Ann, born 3 Nov 1730, daughter of Jacob and Elizabeth (her name was mistakenly listed as Lisby in my 1987 book and Elizabeth's name was not indicated in the parish register)

Lusby, Mary, born 2 Oct 1732, daughter of Jacob and Elizabeth (her name was mistakenly listed as Lisby in my 1987 book and Elizabeth's name was not indicated in the parish register)

Lynch, Anthony and Mary Barton, both of Baltimore County, married 21 Jun 1792 (they were married by virtue of a license issued on 15 Jun 1792; his name was listed as Antony in another part of the parish register)

Lynch, Kidd and Sarah Swarth or Swarts, both of Harford County, married 21 Aug 1791 (her name was mistakenly listed as Sumarts in my 1987 book and as Swasth or Swarth in another part of the parish register; they were married by virtue of the publication of banns)

Lynch, Mary and John Jacobs married 29 Mar 1761 (his name was listed as John Jacob in my 1987 book)

Lynchfield, William and Sarah Parks married 26 Mar 1749 (his name was mistakenly listed as Lunchfield in my 1987 book)

Lyon, Rozannah and Edward Bozman married 27 Feb 1749 (the date should actually be written 27 Feb 1749/50; another entry in the parish register indicated Edward Bosman and Rose Lyon married some time after 11 Feb 1750, but the exact date was not given)

Lyttle, John, son of John and Elizabeth, born 30 Sep 1798, baptized 31 Mar 1799 (his name was listed as Lytle in my 1987 book and his date of baptism was mistakenly listed as 31 Mar 1791)

Macather (Mechliss?), John and Joshua, twin sons of Thomas, born 3 May 1789 (the name Macather looked somewhat like Mechliss, but neither spelling of the name appeared in the marriage records)

Macckelltons, Margaret and John Cameron married 12 Dec 1716 (their names were listed as John Cammeron and Margret Macckelltons in the parish register and in my 1987 book)

Maccomas family names, see "McComas," q.v.

Macdanile, Sarah and Jos. Hawkins married 19 May 1744 (his name was listed as Jos. or Jas. in my 1987 book and her name was probably McDaniel)

Macfee, Malcom and Elizabeth Franklin married in 1775 (the exact date of marriage was not given, but their request to publish marriage banns was entered in the parish register after one dated 10 Aug 1775)

Mackness, John and Elizabeth Morris married in 1751 (the entry in the parish register did not give the exact date)

Macmar, Jane and James Sinkler married 1 Dec 1767 (their names were listed as Jas. Sinkler and Jane McMar in *Maryland Marriages, 1634-1777*)

Macnamara, Mary and James Condon married 17 Apr 1765 (this marriage was entered in the parish register among the 1758 marriages)

Magness, John and Martha Morris married 1 Aug 1799 (they were married by virtue of a license issued on 30 Jul 1799, not 20 Jul 1799 as stated in my 1987 book; his name was also listed as Magnes and Magnus in the parish register, but Magness was the more common spelling)

Mainer, Sarah and Thomas Low married -- Jan 1754 (another entry in the parish register indicated they married subsequent to November, 1753, but the exact date was not given; the earlier date could have been their intention of marriage or publication of banns)

Majors, Elias and Diana Bosley married 8 Sep 1763 (her name was listed as Bozley in my 1987 book)

Mallane, Emanuel and Margrett Reeves married 13 Feb 1749 (the date should actually be written 13 Feb 1749/50; another entry in the parish register indicated Emanuel Mallance or Mallanee and Margaret Reeves married 11 Feb 1750)

Mallane, John and Eddith Cole married 8 Nov 1748 (another entry in the parish register indicated John Mallance or Mallanee and Ediff Cole married 6 Nov 1748)

Malloy, James and Sarah Weeks, both of Harford County, married 13 Aug 1789 (her name was mistakenly listed in my 1987 book as Wicks and their marriage date was listed as 10 Aug 1789; his name was listed as Mulloy in another part of the parish register)

Manby, Edward and Mary Rice married 30 Aug 1761 (his name is difficult to read in the parish register and it could have been Manby or Manley)

March (Marche), John and Hannah Onion, both of Harford County, married 5 Jun 1794 (the parish register indicated they were married by virtue of a license issued in Harford County, but no marriage license was found in Harford or Baltimore County)

March, Thomas and Sophia Carvin married 26 Feb 1744 (the date should actually be written 26 Feb 1744/5; another entry in the parish register indicated Thomas Marsh and Sophia Corbin married 10 Feb 1745; the earlier date could have been their intention of marriage or publication of banns)

Marel, Dinah, see "Dinah Morel," q.v.

Marsh, Thomas, see "Thomas March," q.v.

Marshall, Jacob and Mary Standiford married 5 Jun 1774 (her name was listed as Sandeford and his name as Marshal in my 1987 book)

Martin, Elizabeth and Thomas Yeats married 21 Jun 1744 (another entry in the parish register indicated they married 17 Jun 1744)

Martin, Hannah and Walter Chilson married 16 Jun 1799 (the date was listed as 10 Jun 1799 in another part of the parish register; they were married by virtue of a license issued on 4 Jun 1799; his name was mistakenly listed as Chilsom in my 1987 book; *Maryland Marriages, 1778-1800* indicated the marriage date was 16 Jun 1799)

Martin, Mary and James Scott married 12 Nov 1749 (another entry in the parish register indicated they married some time between 24 Sep and 26 Nov 1749, but the exact date was not given)

Massey, Cassandra and Joseph Woodland married 7 Jul 1772 (her name was listed as Masscey in the parish register)

Matheny, Sarah and Joseph Walton married 28 Apr 1746 (another entry in the parish register indicated they married 23 Mar 1746 and listed her name as Metheny; the earlier date could have been their intention of marriage or publication of banns)

Matthews, Jesse and Ann Conn, both of Harford County, married 1 Aug 1792 (they were married by virtue of a license issued on 30 Jul 1792; his name was listed as Mathews in the parish register)

Maulsby, Maurice and Eleanor Maulsby, both of Harford County, married 22 Mar 1792 (they were married by virtue of a license issued on that same day and listed her name as Elioner)

Maxwell, Ann and John Hammond Dorsey married 20 Jan 1772 (his middle name was listed as Hammon in the parish register)

Maxwell, Moses and Sally Charity Bond, both of Harford County, married 10 Dec 1793 (the parish register indicated they were married by virtue of a license issued in Harford County, but no marriage license was found in Harford or Baltimore County)

McCairman, Nancy and Robert Whiteford, both of Harford County, married 2 Feb 1796 (they were mistakenly listed as Robert Whitfoed and ---- McCarman in my 1987 book; they were married by virtue of a license issued that same day and it listed her name as Nancy Kerman)

McCall, Mary and Anthony Nolman married 1 Aug 1773 (his name was mistakenly listed as Nelman in my 1987 book)

McClean, Andrew and Esther Israel married 2 Dec 1800 (another entry in the parish register indicated Andrew McCleary and Esther Israel were married on 1 Dec 1800)

McCleary, Andrew, see "Andrew McClean," q.v.

McCloughon, Thomas and Deborah King married 10 Jul 1761 (his name was listed as Thos. M'Cloughon and her first name was listed as Deb. in the parish register)

McClung, Adam and Letitia Richardson married 24 Dec 1764 (his name was listed as M'Clong in the parish register)

McComas, Alexander and Elizabeth Day married 19 Nov 1713 (his name was listed as Elecksander Mecomas in my 1987 book)

McComas, Alexander and Hannah Whitaker married 23 Aug 1728 (their names were listed as Alexander Maccomas and Hannah Wittacre in the parish register and in my 1987 book)

McComas, Ann, see "Mary Mccomas," q.v.

McComas, Ann and John Poteet married 20 Apr 1762 (her name was listed as M'Comas in the parish register)

McComas, Aquila and Sarah Preston married 2 Jan 1752 (his name was listed as Aquilla Maccomas in the parish register)

McComas, Daniel (son of Alexander) and Hannah Taylor married 15 Mar 1753 (his name was listed in the parish register as Daniel Maccomas, son Elexander)

McComas, Daniel and Ann Miles married 10 Oct 1758 (his name was listed as Danl. Maccomas in the parish register)

McComas, Daniel and Elizabeth Scott, both of Harford County, married 18 Feb 1796 (they were married by virtue of a license issued that same day)

McComas, Daniel Jr. and Tabitha Johnson married 26 Jan 1743 (his name was listed as Maccomas in the parish register)

McComas, Hannah and Jacob Miles married 10 Nov 1748 (another entry in the parish register indicated they married 6 Nov 1748 and her name was listed as Maccomas)

McComas, James and Elizabeth Hillen married 15 Nov 1761 (his name was entered as Jas. Maccomas in the parish register and her name was listed as Eliz. Hillin)

McComas, James and Sarah Howard, both of Harford County, married 29 May 1794 (the marriage date was mistakenly listed as 29 Mar 1794 in my 1987 book; their marriage license was issued 27 May 1794)

McComas, John, see "Mary Mccomas" and "Sarah McComas," q.v.

McComas, Martha and Parker Gilbert, both of Harford County, married 21 Sep 1797 (they were married by virtue of a license issued on 19 Nov 1797)

McComas, Mary and Samuel Whips married 22 Jan 1742 (their names were listed as Samuel Whipps and Mary Maccomas in my 1987 book)

McComas, Mary, daughter of John and Ann, born 4 Feb 1713 (although her name was misspelled Mecomas and her date of birth was listed as 4 Feb 17-- in my 1987 book, she was noted as Mary McComas, born 4 Feb 1713 in *Baltimore County Families, 1659-1759*)

McComas, Mary, see "Sarah McComas," q.v.

McComas, Nicholas Day and Elizabeth Onion, both of Harford County, married 24 Jul 1794 (they were married by virtue of a license issued in Harford County on 23 Jul 1794 which was noted in the parish register; the marriage license listed his name was N. D. McComas)

McComas, Polly and Patrick Deegan married 24 Oct 1799 (they were married by virtue of a license issued on 23 Oct 1799; his name was mistakenly listed as Dargay in my 1987 book, but it was listed as Deegan in another part of that book)

McComas, Priscilla and Thomas Scimmons married 6 Feb 1753 (her name was listed as Pricilla Maccomas in the parish register)

McComas, Sarah and William Bradford married 16 Feb 1764 (her name was listed as M'Comus in the parish register)

McComas, Sarah, daughter of John and Mary, born 21 Jan 1787 (the year was mistakenly listed as 1781 in my 1987 book)

McComas, William and Elizabeth Scott married 22 Jan 1760 (his name was entered as Maccomus in the parish register)

McCubbin, John and Sarah Holland married 29 Jan 1761 (his name was listed as Jno. M'Cubbin in the parish register)

McCubbin, John and Polley Tudor, both of Baltimore County, married 27 Dec 1791 (her name was listed as Tuder in one part of the parish register; they were married by virtue of a license issued on 24 Dec 1791 which listed her name as Tudor)

McCubbins, Nancy and Isaac Leadley, both of Baltimore County, married 26 Dec 1793 (they were married by virtue of a "licence from Balt. County" as noted in the parish register, but no marriage license was found in Baltimore or Harford County; her name was listed as Mackubbins in another part the parish register)

McCubbins, Susanna and Joshua Tudor, both of Baltimore County, married 9 Oct 1792 (they were married by virtue of a "licence from Balto. County dated instant" as noted in the parish register; the marriage license was issued on 6 Oct 1792 and listed her name as Susannah)

McCullister, Edward and Mary Ryley married 21 Oct 1754 (his name was listed his name as M'Cullister in the parish register)

McDaniel, Sarah, see "Sarah Macdanile," q.v.

McDuggle, James and Eliner Hammond married 28 Jun 1747 (his name was mistakenly listed as James M. Duggle in my 1987 book; *Maryland Marriages, 1634-1777* mistakenly listed his name as James M. M'Duggle)

McGawley, Mary and John Grayham, both of Harford County, married 31 Aug 1787 "by Rev. John Coleman and entered in the parish register of St. John's Parish" (her name was mistakenly listed as McGowley and the minister's name was mistakenly listed as William in my 1987 book)

McGowan, Elizabeth and Thomas Crouch, both of Harford County, married 27 Dec 1790 (although his name was listed as Groush or Gorush in another part of the parish register and they were married by license, no marriage license was found in Harford or Baltimore County; the name was listed as Crouch in my 1987 book and in *Maryland Marriages, 1778-1800*)

McKenly, Allen and Susanna Frissel married 23 Apr 1745 (their names were listed as Mackenley and Freziel in my 1987 book)

McKenly, Elizabeth and Mannus Ocain married 26 Nov 1750 (her name was listed as M'kenly in my 1987 book)

McKenly, Susanna and Daniel Collett married 1 Aug 1749 (her name was listed as Susanah M'kenly in my 1987 book; another entry in the parish register indicated they married 14 May 1749; the earlier date could have been their intention of marriage or publication of banns)

McKinley, Martha and Hezekiah James Balch married 27 -- 1768 (probably married 27 Oct 1768, but the information was incomplete in the parish register; his first name was mistakenly misspelled Hankeah in my 1987 book)

McKinley, Mary and Alexander Stevert (Stovert?) married 11 Dec 1754 (her name was listed as M'Kinley in the parish register)

McLaughlin, Dennis and Mary Dawson, both of Baltimore County, married 18 Dec 1787 (her name was mistakenly listed as Rachel Norris in my 1987 book)

McMath, Samuel and Mary Curry, both of Harford County, married 19 Jun 1792 (the marriage date was mistakenly listed as 18 Jun 1792 in my 1987 book and her name was listed as Cussy in another part of the parish register; they were married by virtue of the publication of banns)

McMath, William and Sarah Moores, both of Harford County, married 11 Dec 1792 (they were married by virtue of a license issued on 11 Nov 1792)

Mead, Edward, see "James Mead," q.v.

Mead, Eleanor, see "Elizabeth Mead," q.v.

Mead, Elizabeth, daughter of Joseph and Eleanor, born 31 Dec 1723 (the name Mead was listed as Meed, Meade, Meads and Meades at various times in the parish register; her date of birth was mistakenly listed as 31 Dec 1719 in my 1987 book)

Mead, James (son of Edward) and Ann Forrest married 21 Dec 1747 (another entry in the parish register indicated James Meads and Anne Forrest married some time between 6 Dec 1747 and 3 Jan 1748, but the exact date was not given)

Mead, Joseph, see "Elizabeth Mead," q.v.

Meads, Elizabeth and John Childs married 4 Dec 1743 (another entry in the parish register indicated John Chields and Elizabeth Mead married 17 Dec 1743; the earlier date could have been their intention of marriage or publication of banns)

Mechliss, Thomas, see "John Macather (Mechliss?)," q.v.

Meds (Meeds?), Margret and John Cammall married 17 Mar 1769 (her name was listed incorrectly as Msds. in my 1987 book)

Menson, Richard and Mary Ward married 24 Mar 1763 (his name was listed in the parish register as either Rd. Menson or Rd. Minson)

Mercer, John and Rebecca Judy married 28 Feb 1765 (another entry in the parish register indicated that Rev. Hugh Deans, Rector of St. John's Parish in Baltimore County, was authorized on 18 Feb 1765 by the Honorable Horatio Sharpe, Governor of Maryland, to solemnize the marriage of John Marcer and Rebecca Judah according to law)

Merriken, Elizabeth, wife of Joshua Merriken, died 17 Dec 1716 (the name was also listed as Merrica, Marrica, Merrken and Merrikeen at various times in the parish register)

Merriken, Joshua, see "Elizabeth Merriken," q.v.

Merryman, Elizabeth and Jethro Lynch Wilkinson married 29 Jan 1761 (her name was listed as Eliz. Marryman in the parish register)

Merryman, Elizabeth and Elisha Bosley married 29 Jun 1769 (his name was listed as Bozley in my 1987 book)

Merryman, Nicholas and Avarilla Raven married 1 May 1755 (her name was listed as Reaven in the parish register)

Middlemore, Josias and Frances Bochley or Bechley married 9 Oct 1720 (their names were listed as Josias Midlemore and Frances Bochley or Bechley in my 1987 book)

Middleton, John and Mary Cowan, both of Harford County, married 15 Sep 1793 (they were married by virtue of a license issued on 28 Aug 1793)

Miles, Ann and Daniel McComas married 10 Oct 1758 (his name was listed as Danl. Maccomas in the parish register)

Miles, Jacob and Hannah McComas married 10 Nov 1748 (another entry in the parish register indicated they married 6 Nov 1748 and her name was listed as Maccomas)

Milhughs, Aquilla and Elizabeth Parks married 17 Dec 1749 (another entry in the parish register listed their names as Aquila Milhuse and Elizabeth Parkes)

Milhughs, Brigett and John Parks married 29 Oct 1743 (her name was listed once in the parish register as Bridget Milhews and mistakenly listed as Wilhughs in my 1987 book; another entry in the parish register indicated they married 11 Sep 1743; the earlier date could have been their intention of marriage or publication of banns)

Milhughs, Frances and Thomas Cottrall married 31 Jul 1743 (her name was mistakenly listed as Williams in my 1987 book; another entry in the parish register indicated their names were Thomas Cotteraell and Frances Milhuse and they married 4 Aug 1743; their names were listed as Thomas Cotterel and Frances Millhughes in *Maryland Marriages, 1634-1777*)

Milhughs, Sabra and John Ash married 8 Feb 1763 (her name was misspelled Sabre in my 1987 book)

Miller, Theophilus, see "Thos. Miller," q.v.

Miller, Thos. and Sarah Burk married 24 Jul 1748 (another entry in the parish register indicated they married in July 1748, but the exact date was not given; his name was listed as Theophilus instead of Thomas in my 1987 book)

Millikin, Susanna and Asael Barton, both of Baltimore County, married 27 Dec 1791 ("codem die ambo 27th Dec." was written above their names in the parish register; they were married by virtue of a license issued on 20 Dec 1791 which listed her name as Susannah Milliken)

Mills, Mary and Bond James Kimboley, both of Harford County, married 11 Sep 1787 (his name was mistakenly listed as Kimbley in my 1987 book)

Minson, Mary and James Steadman married 10 Oct 1747 (her name was mistakenly listed as Munson in my 1987 book; *Maryland Marriages, 1634-1777* has listed both marriage dates and listed her name once as Misnon, an apparent typographical error; another entry in the parish register indicated James Steedman and Mary Minson married 23 Aug 1747; the earlier date could have been their intention of marriage or publication of banns)

Minson, Richard, see "Richard Menson," q.v.

Minson, Sarah, see "Sarah Nixon," q.v.

Mitchell, Avarilla and Robert Hawkins married 19 May 1772 (their names were mistakenly listed as Robert Hawlines and Arebella Mitchel in the parish register and in my 1987 book)

Mitchell, Jane and George Carrothers married 18 Feb 1768 (their names in the parish register appeared to be Geo. Carrothus and Jane Mitchl. and this was noted as such in *Maryland Marriages, 1634-1777*)

Mitchell, Sarah and Isaac Low married 5 Nov 1761 (his name was spelled Lowe in my 1987 book)

Miver, William and Elizabeth Finer married 10 Oct 1748 (another entry in the parish register indicated William Miver and Isabell Fara married 4 Sep 1748; the earlier date could have been their intention of marriage or publication of banns; *Maryland Marriages, 1634-1777* listed them as two separate marriages)

Miyon, Margaretta and Christian Monts married 30 Mar 1755 (his name was listed as Christison and her name was misspelled Margraretta in my 1987 book)

Moffett, Hannah and Daniel Ruff married 31 Dec 1801 (they were married by virtue of a license issued on 8 Dec 1801; her name was listed as Maffitt in another part of the parish register and in my 1987 book)

Monks, Anna Bella, daughter of John and Mary, born 12 Sep 1789 (her name was listed as Anne Belle in my 1987 book)

Monks, Elicia, daughter of John and Mary, born 25 Jan 1795 (her name was listed as Elican Monks in my 1987 book)

Monks, William, son of John and Mary, born 2 Jan 1787 (the date was listed as 6 Jan 1787 in my 1987 book)

Montgomery, Anne, daughter of William and Margaret, born 15 Feb 1745 (her name was listed as Megummery in my 1987 book)

Montgomery, Jane and James Dobson married 1 Jul 1745 (another entry in the parish register indicated they married 23 Jun 1745 and listed her name as Mongumry)

Monts, Christian and Margaretta Miyon married 30 Mar 1755 (his name was listed as Christison and her name was misspelled Margraretta in my 1987 book)

Moore, John and Mary Scarborough, both of Harford County, married 3 Aug 1797 (her name was listed as Scarborough in the parish register; a marriage license was issued on 3 Aug 1797 and listed her name as Scarbrough)

Moore, Mary and Groombright Bayley married 5 Oct 1757 (his name was listed as Groome Bright Bayley in the parish register and in my 1987 book)

Moore, Philip and Delia(h) Hall, both of Baltimore County, married 30 Apr 1799 (another entry in the parish register indicated they married on 13 Apr 1799; *Maryland Marriages, 1778-1800* indicated they married on 30 Apr 1799; no marriage license was found in Baltimore or Harford County to verify the date, so the earlier date could have been their intention of marriage or publication of banns)

Moores, Daniel and Sarah Budd, both of Harford County, married 1 Jan 1793 (they were married by virtue of a license issued on 3 Dec 1792 and listed her name as Sally)

Moores, Sarah and William McMath, both of Harford County, married 11 Dec 1792 (they were married by virtue of a license issued on 11 Nov 1792)

Morel, Dinah and Thomas Hobeard married 3 Mar 1771 (her name was listed as Marel in my 1987 book)

Morgan, James and Mary Green married 12 Nov 1749 (another entry in the parish register indicated they married between 24 Sep and 26 Nov 1749, but the exact date was not given)

Morris, Edward, see "John Morris," q.v.

Morris, Elizabeth and John Mackness married in 1751 (the entry in the parish register did not give the exact date)

Morris, John and Sarah Gilbert married 31 Jul 1743 (another entry in the parish register indicated they married 28 Aug 1743)

Morris, John (son of Edward) and Mary Beaver married 25 Feb 1768 (his name was listed as "Jno. Morris, son Edward" in the parish register)

Morris, Martha and John Magness married 1 Aug 1799 (they were married by virtue of a license issued on 30 Jul 1799, not 20 Jul 1799 as stated in my 1987 book; his name was also listed as Magnes and Magnus in the parish register, but Magness was the more common spelling)

Morris, Sarah and John Jones married 28 Mar 1749 (another entry in the parish register indicated "John Jones and Sarah Morris this court married" subsequent to 26 Mar 1749, but the exact date was not given)

Morris, Thomas and Frances Shaw married 10 Oct 1749 (another entry in the parish register indicated they married some time between 24 Sep and 26 Nov 1749, but the exact date was not given)

Morrow, Susanna and Oliver Harriott married 17 Jan 1717 (their names were listed as Oliver Harrett and Susannah Morrow in my 1987 book)

Moss, Elizabeth and William Bowen married 16 Sep 1753 (another entry in the parish register indicated they married in 1753, but the exact date was not given and his name was listed as Bowing)

Moulins, John, see "John Mullen," q.v.

Mullen, John and Sarah Brown married 16 Jan 1743 (the date should actually be written 16 Jan 1743/4; another entry in the parish register indicated John Moulins and Sarah Brown married 15 Jan 1743)

Mulner, Charles and Cassandra Chamberlaine married 7 Jan 1773 (her name was listed as Casander Chamberlane in my 1987 book)

Murphy, James and Sarah Cheyne married 9 Nov 1746 (another entry in the parish register indicated James Murphey and Sarah Chainy married 15 Dec 1746; the earlier date could have been their intention of marriage or publication of banns)

Murphy, Margret and William Dortridge married 19 Oct 1749 (another entry in the parish register indicated William Dawdrege and Margaret Murphey married 3 Sep 1749; the earlier date could have been their intention of marriage or publication of banns)

Murray, Elizabeth and Robert Peak, both of Harford County, married 27 Sep 1789 (her name was listed as Murrey in another part of the parish register)

Murray, Hannah and Thomas Brown, both of Baltimore County, married 29 Jul 1793 (they were married by virtue of the publication of banns; her name was listed as Murrey in my 1987 book)

Murray, Rebecca and Richard Cook married 9 Nov 1769 (her name was listed as Rebeca Murrey in my 1987 book)

Myers, Elizabeth and Charles Hipkins, both of Baltimore County, married 10 May 1789 (her name was listed as Mires in my 1987 book, but it was listed as Myers and Myres in different parts of the parish register)

Nairn (Nearn), Elizabeth and Ambrose Leech married 7 Jul 1748 (another entry in the parish register listed their names as Ambross Leach and Elizabeth Nearn and their marriage date was mistakenly indicated as 5 Jul 1749 in my 1987 book)

Nairne (Nearn), Ann(e) and Richard Williams married 12 Jun 1746 (another entry in the parish register gave the same information, but listed her name as Ann Nearn)

Nairne (Nearn), Robert and Ann Lerman married 29 Oct 1724 (her name was listed as Larman in my 1987 book)

Nash, Thomas and Lucretia Weeks, both of Harford County, married 25 Dec 1788 (her name was mistakenly listed as Wicks in my 1987 book)

Neill, Ann and Thomas Sheredine, both of Harford County, married 9 Mar 1797 (they were married by virtue of a license issued on 19 Mar 1797; her name was listed as Neil in the parish register)

Neill, William and Mary Sheredine, both of Harford County, married 2 Nov 1797 (they were married by virtue of a license issued on that same day)

Nelson, John and Frances Rhodes married 15 Nov 1715 (her last name was not indicated in the parish register, but *Baltimore County Families, 1659-1759* indicated John Nelson and Frances Rhodes married 12 Jan 1718; his name was listed as Nellson in my 1987 book and the parish register was difficult to read, but the date was clearly 15 Nov 1715)

Nesbitt, Isabella and John Powell married 24 Oct 1799 (they were married by virtue of a license issued on 15 Oct 1799; her name was listed as Isabell Nasbitt in another part of the parish register and in my 1987 book)

Newman, Ann(e) and Simon Hutcheson married 24 Aug 1746 (another entry in the parish register indicated Simon Hutchinson and Ann Newman married 25 Aug 1746)

News, Timothy and Sarah Beaver married 13 Dec 1764 (his name was mistakenly listed as New in my 1987 book)

Nichols, Drucilla, see "Sarah Nichols," q.v.

Nichols, Drusilla Durbin and Isaac Kelly married 2 Apr 1801 (their names were listed as Kelley and Nicolls in another part of the parish register)

Nichols, Frances and David Asquith, both of Baltimore County, married 2 Oct 1791 (the parish register indicated they were married by virtue of a license issued in Harford County, but no marriage license was found in Harford or Baltimore County)

Nichols, Hannah and Charles Jones married 26 Dec 1752 (another entry in the parish register indicated they married in 1752, but the exact date was not given, and her name was listed as Nicholes)

Nichols, James, see "Sarah Nichols," q.v.

Nichols, Lucretia, see "Sarah Nichols," q.v.

Nichols, Sarah, daughter of James and Drucilla, born 15 Aug 1758 (her date of birth was incomplete in my 1987 book and it was entered as "15 Aug 1750?" in *Baltimore County Families, 1659-1759*; it could have been 1758 since the only other known child of James and Drucilla was a daughter Lucretia born 25 Sep 1760; the date of marriage of James and Drucilla Nichols was also not indicated)

Nichols, Thomas and Frances James married 21 Aug 1740 (this marriage was entered in the parish register among the 1744 marriages)

Nichols, Thomas and Prissella Back (Bank) married 10 Feb 1763 (her name was difficult to read in the parish register and it could have been Back, Bank or Banks)

Nicholson, James and Dricella Durbin married 24 Dec 1757 (her name was mistakenly listed as Ducella in my 1987 book)

Niel, Thomas and Mary Wagstar married -- Apr 1748 (the exact date of marriage was not given, but the entry in the parish register indicated they married subsequent to 3 Apr 1748; *Maryland Marriages, 1634-1777* listed the marriage as "Thomas Niel and Mary Wagstar, April 1747, banns. pub. three times")

Nixon (Nixion), Sarah and Christoher Dives married 24 Jun 1762 (his first name was listed as Chris. in the parish register; her last name was difficult to read and could have been Nixon, Nixion or Minson)

Nolman, Anthony and Mary McCall married 1 Aug 1773 (his name was mistakenly listed as Nelman in my 1987 book)

Norrington, Francis and Mary Everett or Everitt married 19 Feb 1749 (another entry in the parish register indicated they married subsequent to 11 Feb 1750, but the exact date was not given)

Norrington, John and Mary Hays married 1 Aug 1737 (his name was listed as Norrinton in my 1987 book)

Norris, Ann and Benjamin Lony married 7 May 1745 (his name was mistakenly listed as Long in my 1987 book)

Norris, Benjamin and Sarah Whitaker married 8 Oct 1719 (her last name was not indicated in the parish register and in my 1987 book, but *Baltimore County Families, 1659-1759* indicated her name was Whitaker)

Norris, Elizabeth and Ezekiel Bosley married 21 Oct 1760 (his name was listed as Ezikiel Bozley in the parish register)

Norris, Hannah (of Harford County) and Joseph Scott, Jr. (of Baltimore County) married 5 Mar 1795 (his name was inadvertently listed without the Jr. in my 1987 book; they were married by virtue of a license issued in Baltimore County on 4 Mar 1795)

Norris, John and Martha Long married 12 Nov 1772 (her name was mistakenly listed as Marth in my 1987 book)

Norris, Martha and Enoch Churchman, of Baltimore County, married 2 Feb 1792 (they were married by virtue of a license from Harford County as noted in the parish register; the license was issued on 1 Feb 1792)

Norris, Mary and John Shoebridge married 28 Oct 1732 (the date of marriage was mistakenly listed as 28 Sep 1732 and her surname was misspelled as Morris in my 1987 book; his name was listed as Shewbridge in other parts of the parish register)

Norris, Rachael and Gist Vaughan married 2 Mar 1769 (his name was misspelled Vaugham in my 1987 book)

Norris, Rachel and Thomas Chinworth, both of Harford County, married 1 Jan 1788 (her last name was inadvertently omitted from my 1987 book)

Norris, Sarah and Asael Hitchcock, Asael married 8 Oct 1742 (another entry in the parish register indicated they married 8 Oct 1741)

Norris, Susanna and Richard Atherton married 1 Nov 1721 (*Maryland Marriages, 1634-1777* indicated they married 1 Nov 1729, yet their marriage was entered in the parish register among the 1721-1722 marriages)

Norris, Susannah and Walter Wyle married 29 Dec 1763 (his name was written as Walt. Wyle in the parish register)

Norris, Wheelamina and Vincent Bosley married 28 Mar 1771 (his name was listed as Bozley in my 1987 book)

Norton, John and Sarah Jones, both of Harford County, married 20 Sep 1789 (their marriage date was mistakenly listed as 24 Sep 1789 in my 1987 book)

Nusewonden, Daniel and Sarah Asher married 14 Nov 1761 (his name as mistakenly listed as Nuservonden in my 1987 book)

Nutterville, Araminta and George Debrular, both of Harford County, married 12 Jul 1791 (although her name looked like Aminta Nutterwell in the parish register, a marriage license issued 11 Jul 1791 listed their names as George Debruler and Aramenta Nutterville)

O'Brian, Thomas and Amelia Woolling married 14 Jun 1757 (his name was listed as Thos. Obrian in the parish register)

O'Bryan, John and Ellinor Jackson (widow) married 24 Sep 1721 (they were listed as John Bryan and Elinor Jackson in *Maryland Marriages, 1634-1777*)

O'Henry, Henry and Ann Price, both of Harford County, married 27 Jul 1797 (their marriage date was mistakenly listed as 27 Jul 1791 in *Maryland Marriages, 1778-1800*; they were issued a marriage license on 27 Jul 1797 and married the same day)

O'Neall, Daniel and Susanna Lacey married 12 Jun 1743 (their names were listed as Daniel Oneall and Sunsannah Lacy in my 1987 book)

Oakdin, John, see "John Oggdon," q.v.

Ocain, Mannus and Elizabeth McKenly married 26 Nov 1750 (her name was listed as M'kenly in my 1987 book)

Odean, Eleanor and John Durbin married 13 Dec 1743 (her name was listed as Elioner Odan in *Maryland Marriages, 1634-1777*)

Oggdon, John and Susannah Harps married 19 Nov 1748 (another entry in the parish register indicated they married 23 Oct 1748 and his name was listed as Oakdin; the earlier date could have been their intention of marriage or publication of banns)

Onion, Elizabeth and Nicholas Day McComas, both of Harford County, married 24 Jul 1794 (they were married by virtue of a license issued in Harford County on 23 Jul 1794 which was noted in the parish register; the marriage license listed his name was N. D. McComas)

Onion, Hannah and John March or Marche, both of Harford County, married 5 Jun 1794 (the parish register indicated they were married by virtue of a license issued in Harford County, but no marriage license was found in Harford or Baltimore County)

Osborn, Benjamin, son of Samuel and Mary, born 19 Mar 1777, died -- Feb 1781 (the year was listed as 1785 in my 1987 book, but it could have been 1781)

Osborn, Samuel Groome and Sarah Waltham married 4 Jan 1784 (this marriage was entered in the parish register among the 1754 marriages)

Otherson (Othasson), Rebecca and John Wright, both of Harford County, married 21 Aug 1791 (although her name was listed as Othasson in the parish register, a marriage license issued in Baltimore County on 17 Aug 1791 listed her name as Otherson)

Owen, John and Permelie Cheyne married 12 Nov 1761 (her name was listed as Parmelie in my 1987 book)

Owings, Mary (of Baltimore County) and Richard Cromwell (of Anne Arundel County) married 6 Feb 1800 (this information was omitted from my 1987 book)

Paca, ----, son of Aquila and Martha, born 28 Oct 1703 (although his first name was not indicated in my 1987 book and his date of birth was listed as 28 Oct 1703, he was noted as an unnamed son of Aquila Paca, born 28 Oct 1701, in *Baltimore County Families, 1659-1759*; however, this was an apparent typographical error since Aquila Paca had a daughter Mary born 14 Sep 1701 and two year's later a son was born 28 Oct 1703 as noted in the parish register)

Paca, Susanna (Mrs.) of Baltimore County and Joseph Galloway of Anne
Arundel County married 18 Oct 1722 (the Mrs. was omitted from her name
in my 1987 book)

Packcow, Hannah, see "Hannah Peckon," q.v.

Pakt (Pak't), Elizabeth and Samuel Chamberlaine married 24 Oct 1771 (their
names were listed as Samuel Chamberlane and Elizabeth Pakt in my 1987
book and as Samuel Chamberlaine and Eliza. Pak't in *Maryland Marriages,
1634-1777*)

Palmer, George and Mary Tipper married 30 Aug 1761 (her name was difficult
to read in the parish register and it could have been Tipper or Tapper)

Palmer, Hannah and John Gebbs married 1 Jan 1751 (another entry in the parish
register indicated they married in 1751, but the exact date was not given, and
his name was listed as Gibbs)

Palmer, John and Lidie Collins married 5 Nov 1769 (her name was listed as
Sidie or Lidie in my 1987 book)

Parish, Benjamin and Nancy Hunter, both of Baltimore County, married 1 Mar
1792 (they were married by virtue of a license issued on 18 Feb 1792)

Parish, Jean, see "Jane Parrish," q.v.

Parker, Elizabeth and Artura Conelly married 17 Oct 1770 (her name was listed
as Eliz. in the parish register)

Parker, John and Elizabeth Danbie married 1 Jan 1739 (another entry in the
parish register indicated John Parker and Mary Danbe married on this date)

Parker, Mary and William Bennett married 6 Feb 1753 (another entry in the
parish register indicated they married in 1753, but the exact date was not
given)

Parker, Robert and Mary Copas married 29 Nov 1762 (her name was difficult to
read in the parish register and it could have been Copas or Capas)

Parkew (Parken), Martha and Emanuel Jones married 14 Aug 1757 (her name
could have been spelled either Parkew or Parken in the parish register)

Parkinson, Mary, see "Mary Perkinson," q.v.

Parks, Elizabeth and Aquilla Milhughs married 17 Dec 1749 (another entry in
the parish register listed their names as Aquila Milhuse and Elizabeth
Parkes)

Parks, John and Brigett Milhughs married 29 Oct 1743 (her name was listed
once in the parish register as Bridget Milhews and mistakenly listed as
Wilhughs in my 1987 book; another entry in the parish register indicated
they married 11 Sep 1743; the earlier date could have been their intention of
marriage or publication of banns)

Parks, John and Kezia Rutledge married 3 Nov 1761 (her name was mistakenly
listed as Lezia in my 1987 book)

Parks, Philip and Hannah Peckon married 14 Dec 1746 (another entry in the
parish register indicated Phillip Parks and Hannah Packcow married 22 Dec
1746)

Parks, Sarah and William Lynchfield married 26 Mar 1749 (his name was
mistakenly listed as Lunchfield in my 1987 book)

Parrish, Jane and Samuel Smith married 31 Dec 1743 (another entry in the parish register indicated they married 18 Dec 1743 and her name was listed as Jean Parish; the earlier date could have been their intention of marriage or publication of banns)

Parrish, Benjamin, see "Benjamin Parish," q.v.

Parsley, Israel and Sarah Cheyrton married 5 Feb 1743 (the date should actually be written 5 Feb 1743/4; another entry in the parish register indicated Israel Pasley and Sarah Cheverton married 22 Jan 1744; the earlier date could have been their intention of marriage or publication of banns)

Pasmore, Mary and John Dunnock married 16 Jan 1743 (the date should actually be written 16 Jan 1742/3; his name was mistakenly listed as Dannock and her name as Palmore in my 1987 book; another entry in the parish register indicated John Dunnike and Mary Pasmore married 5 Dec 1742; the earlier date could have been their intention of marriage or publication of banns)

Pasmore, Rebecca and Thomas Wodgworth married -- Jan 1741 (his name was listed as Wordgworth in other parts of the parish register)

Peacock, Anne and William Smith married -- Dec 1751 (the complete date was not given in the parish register)

Peacocke, John and Anne Higgins married -- May 1747 (the entry in the parish register indicated they married some time between 10 May and 17 May 1747, but the exact date was not given)

Peaifers (Peaiters), Ann and John Bickerton (Bixerton) married circa 1765 (the exact date of marriage was not given, but their request to publish marriage banns was entered in the parish register some time between 28 Apr 1765 and 20 Jul 1766; John's name was listed as Bickerton and Bixerton in the parish register; Ann had an unusual last name which may have been either Peaifers or Peaiters)

Peak, Robert and Elizabeth Murray, both of Harford County, married 27 Sep 1789 (her name was listed as Murrey in another part of the parish register)

Pearson, Simon, see "Simon Person," q.v.

Peckon, Hannah and Philip Parks married 14 Dec 1746 (another entry in the parish register indicated Phillip Parks and Hannah Packcow married 22 Dec 1746)

Pendergest, Luke and Rachel Simmons married 26 Jan 1768 (his name was mistakenly listed as Luke Pinder Gist in my 1987 book)

Pennington, Elizabeth and George Sunk married 23 Sep 1766 (this entry in the parish register was actually listed as "Geo. Sunk & Eliz. Pennenton, Eliz. Pennington marrd. Sep 23d 1766")

Perdue, Elizabeth and John Wyle married 12 May 1748 (another entry in the parish register indicated John Wiley and Elizabeth Perdue married 3 Apr 1748; the earlier date could have been their intention of marriage or publication of banns)

Perdue, Mary and Thomas Anderson married 26 Mar 1744 (another entry in the parish register indicated they married 18 Mar 1744)

Perdue, William and Rebecca Low or Lowe married 4 Feb 1747 (the date should actually be written 4 Feb 1747/8; another entry in the parish register indicated they married subsequent to 31 Jan 1748, but the exact date was not given)

Perigoe, Henry and Providence Corbin married 14 Jan 1745 (the date should actually be written 14 Jan 1745/6; another entry in the parish register indicated they married 24 Nov 1745; the earlier date could have been their intention of marriage or publication of banns)

Perkins, Priscilla and Jacob Fulks, both of Baltimore County, married 13 Dec 1792 (no marriage license was found in Balimore or Harford County so they were apparently married by virtue of the publication of banns)

Perkinson, Mary and Joseph Ward married 13 Feb 1748 (the date should actually be 13 Feb 1748/9; another entry in the parish register indicated they married subsequent to 3 Feb 1749, but the exact date was not given, and her name was listed as Parkinson)

Perry, Alice and John Strickland, both of Harford County, married 30 Jun 1793 (they were married by virtue of the publication of banns)

Person, Simon and Sarah Shaw married 2 Feb 1715 (her name was spelled Schaw and his name was listed as Symon Person and Simon Pearson at various times in the parish register and in my 1987 book)

Petetow, Mary and John Whicks married 24 Jan 1765 (his name in the parish register appeared to be either Jno. Whicks or Wheeks)

Petty, Ann(e) and Thomas Underwood married 31 Jul 1743 (another entry in the parish register indicated they married 1 Aug 1743)

Petty, Ann(e) and John Thompson married 7 Jul 1748 (another entry in the parish register indicated they married in July 1748, but the exact date was not given)

Phillips, Elizabeth and Joseph Brooks married 28 May 1747 (another entry in the parish register indicated they married 1 Jun 1747)

Phipps, Nathan and Rebecca Davies, both of Harford County, married 29 Jan 1789 (his name was listed as Phips in my 1987 book)

Phraisher, Kezia, see "Kezia Fraisher," q.v.

Pickett, Heathcot and Elizabeth Wright married 26 Jan 1742 (his name was misspelled Heathcut in my 1987 book and their names were listed as Heathcote Pickett and Eliz. Wright in *Maryland Marriages, 1634-1777*)

Pickett, John and Pemela Dukes married 3 Oct 1756 (his name was listed as Jno. in the parish register and her name was listed as Pemela or Pernela in my 1987 book)

Pickett, Mary and Deowald Heldebroad married 8 Jul 1753 (although it appeared to be Heldebroad in the parish register his name could have been Hildebrand)

Pinix, Sarah and William Linam, both of Harford County, married 17 Dec 1797 (her name was listed as Pinox in my 1987 book; they were married by virtue of a license issued on 5 Dec 1797 and listed her name as Pinix)

Pinkstone, William and Ann Inmon or Lumon married -- Oct 1743 (her name was listed as Inman in my 1987 book and as Lumon in *Maryland Marriages, 1634-1777*)

Plant, Margaret and James Clarke married in 1753 (the complete date was not given in the parish register)

Pocock, Elizabeth and Skelton Standiford, Jr. married 4 Nov 1755 (her name was listed as Eliz. in the parish register and his name as Standeford in the my 1987 book)

Pocock, Susan and Ephraim Rutledge married 6 Feb 1766 (his name was listed as Eprmarried and her name was listed as Poccock in the parish register)

Poess, Rd. Sister(?) and Johannah Thomas married 4 Sep 1763 (his most unsual name was written in the parish register as either Rd. Sister Poess or Rd. Lister Poess and it remains an identification problem)

Pollard, Roannah and John Slater married 18 Aug 1755 (her name was difficult to read in the parish register and it could have been Roannah or Rosannah)

Pollard, William and Mary Hildebrand married 19 May 1755 (her name was difficult to read in the parish register and it could have been Hildebrand or Heldebroad)

Pollet, William and Elizabeth Hill married in 1753 (the complete date was not given in the parish register)

Polson, Ann and Joseph Rhodous married -- Jun 1725 (their names were listed as shown in my 1987 book, but her name was listed as Polion in *Maryland Marriages, 1634-1777*)

Polson, Francis, see "Francis Poulson," q.v.

Poor, James and Sarah Elliot married in 1747 (the complete date was not given in the parish register)

Poor, Nicholas, see "Nicholas Power," q.v.

Porrord, Mary, see "Mary Forrord (Porrord)," q.v.

Poteet, Ann and Abraham Whitaker married 15 Jul 1725 (their names were listed as Abraham Wittacre and Ann Puttee in the parish register)

Poteet, Elizabeth and Charles Scimmons married 19 Oct 1742 (another entry in the parish register listed their names as Charles Scimmons and Elizabeth Poteett; his name was mistakenly listed as Summons in my 1987 book and her name was misspelled Pottet; *Maryland Marriages, 1634-1777* listed his name as Simmons)

Poteet, John and Ann McComas married 20 Apr 1762 (her name was listed as M'Comas in the parish register)

Poteet, Lewis, see "Lewis Puttee," q.v.

Potett, Piercey and Jemima Hitchcock married 12 Oct 1743 (his name was listed as Potelt in *Maryland Marriages, 1634-1777*)

Poulson, Francis and Mary Dennock married 13 Feb 1749 (the date should actually be written 13 Feb 1748/9; another entry in the parish register indicated Francis Polson and Mary Dennick married some time between November 1748 and February 1749, but the exact date was not given)

Poulson, John and Elizabeth Stewart married 8 Apr 1750 (another entry in the parish register indicated John Boulson and Elizabeth Steward married in 1750, but the exact date was not given)

Poulson, Sarah and John Jones married 14 Jul 1748 (another entry in the parish register indicated they married subsequent to 7 Jul 1748, but the exact date was not given; the marriage date was mistakenly listed as 14 Jul 1749 in my 987 book)

Powell, John and Isabella Nesbitt married 24 Oct 1799 (they were married by virtue of a license issued on 15 Oct 1799; her name was listed as Isabell Nasbitt in another part of the parish register and in my 1987 book)

Powell, Sarah and William Harman married 24 Jun 1744 (another entry in the parish register indicated William Harmon and Sarah Powel married 17 Jun 1744)

Power, Nicholas and Elizabeth Erickson married 6 Jan 1753 (his name was listed in the parish register as Nichs. Poor, but subsequent research indicated his name was actually Nicholas Power)

Presbury, Joseph and Mrs. Eleanor Carlisle married 11 Jul 1723 (their names were listed as Joseph Presbury and Mrs. Elinor Ca---- in my 1987 book and as Joseph Presbury and Eleanor Carlisle in *Maryland Marriages, 1634-1777*)

Presbury, Mary and William Weatherel, both of Harford County, married 21 Sep 1797 (his name was listed as William Witherall in my 1987 book; a marriage license was issued to William Weatherall and Mary Presbury on 19 Sep 1797)

Presbury, Thomas and Ann Woodard married -- Dec 1749 (this marriage was entered in the parish register among the December, 1750 marriages)

Preston, Daniel and Ann Rigdon married 28 May 1772 (his name was mistakenly listed as Dreston in my 1987 book)

Preston, James and Elizabeth Pritchard married -- Oct 1713 (her name was listed as Pritcherd in my 1987 book)

Preston, Milly, see "Milly Proctor," q.v.

Preston, Sarah and Aquila McComas married 2 Jan 1752 (his name was listed as Aquilla Maccomas in the parish register)

Price, Ann and Henry O'Henry, both of Harford County, married 27 Jul 1797 (they were issued a marriage license that same day; the date of marriage was mistakenly listed as 27 Jul 1791 in *Maryland Marriages, 1778-1800*)

Price, James and Eleanor Carroll married 15 Apr 1770 (her name was listed as Elinor Carrol in the parish register)

Price, Thomas, see "Vissey Price," q.v.

Price, Vissey and Sim. Barton married 19 Oct 1769 (he was probably the Veazey Price who was listed with Thomas Price as a taxable in Back Creek Hundred in Cecil County in 1766 and the Veazy Price who was a non-juror to the Oath of Allegiance in Baltimore County in 1778; her complete first name was not indicated in the parish register, but it may have been Semelia)

Prigg, William and Jane Carson married 27 Jan 1745 (the date should actually be written 27 Jan 1745/6; another entry in the parish register indicated they married 26 Jan 1746 and listed her name as Jean Carsan)

Prine, Peter and Hannah Amoss married 13 Nov 1760 (his name was listed as Prynne in the parish register and in my 1987 book)

Pring, James and Rachel Riset married in 1753 (the complete date was not given in the parish register)

Prington, Yorinth and Jonathan Procter married 30 Jul 1772 (her name was mistakenly listed as Gorinth in my 1987 book)

Pritchard, Elizabeth and James Preston married -- Oct 1713 (her name was listed as Pritcherd in my 1987 book)

Procter, Jonathan and Yorinth Prington married 30 Jul 1772 (her name was mistakenly listed as Gorinth in my 1987 book)

Proctor, Milly and Benjamin Carroll, both of Harford County, married 25 Dec 1792 (his name was listed as Carrol in the parish register and although her name appeared to be Milly Preston it was listed as Mills Proctor in my 1987 book and in *Maryland Marriages, 1778-1800*; however, no marriage license was found in Baltimore or Harford County to verify the spelling because they were married by virtue of the publication of banns)

Prosper, Susan and Richard Rhodes married 16 Apr 1769 (his name was listed as Rodes in the parish register)

Prosser, Charles and Margaret Simkins married 27 Sep 1753 (another entry in the parish register indicated they married in 1753, but the exact date was not given and her name was listed as Margrett Synkins)

Puttee, Ann, see "Ann Poteet," q.v.

Puttee, Lewis and Catherine Green married 12 Jun 1722 (his name was listed as Lewis Poteet in *Maryland Marriages, 1634-1777*)

Quinley, James and Mary Garritt married 26 May 1761 (his name was difficult to read in the parish register and it could have been Quinley or Quinby)

Rampley, James and Sarah Gibson married 22 Sep 1771 (his name was listed as Rumpley in my 1987 book)

Ramsey, Margret and Lewes Demorse married 6 Jan 1743 (the date should actually be written 6 Jan 1743/4; another entry in the parish register indicated Lewis Demors of Opecan and Margaret Ramsey of this parish married 1 Jan 1744; his name was listed as Demoss in other parts of the parish register)

Ramsey, Susannah and John Demorse married 2 Feb 1743 (the date should actually be written 2 Feb 1743/4; his name was listed as Demoss in other parts of the parish register; another entry in the parish register indicated John Demors of Opecan and Susanna Ramsey of this parish married 1 Jan 1744; the earlier date could have been their intention of marriage or publication of banns)

Ramsey, Susannah and Henry Wood married 3 Nov 1766 (her last name was not listed in the parish register when they were married, but it was listed when their request to publish marriage banns was entered in the parish register on 20 Jul 1766)

Raven, Avarilla and Nicholas Merryman married 1 May 1755 (her name was listed as Reaven in the parish register)

Raven, Elizabeth and Charles Harryman married 6 Feb 1752 (her name was listed as Reaven in the parish register)

Raven, Esther and Robert Dew married 3 Oct 1754 (her name was listed as Easther Reaven in the parish register)

Raven, Letitia and Josias Reeves married 11 Jan 1756 (her name was listed as Reaven in the parish register)

Raven, Luke and Ann Rigbie married 20 Aug 1765 (his name was listed a Reaven in the parish register)

Raven, Mary and Richardson Stansbury married 23 Feb 1747 (her name was listed as Reaven in the parish register)

Raven, Mary and James Brian married 4 Jul 1754 (her name was listed as Reaven in the parish register)

Raven, Sarah and John Cotterel married 10 Mar 1763 (her name was listed as Reaven in the parish register)

Raven, Sarah and George Harryman married 17 Oct 1749 (her name was listed as Reaven in the parish register)

Read, Edward and Susannah Shelly married in 1771 (the exact date of marriage was not given, but their request to publish marriage banns was entered in the parish register on 15 Sep 1771)

Reaves, William and Martha Stevens married in summer of 1742 (her name was actually entered as "Martha Stevens Quart." in the parish register)

Reed, Rebecca and Thomas Rock, both of Harford County, married 29 May 1791 (they were married by virtue of the publication of banns)

Reeves, Josias and Letitia Raven married 11 Jan 1756 (her name was listed as Reaven in the parish register)

Reeves, Margrett and Emanuel Mallane married 13 Feb 1749 (the date should actually be written 13 Feb 1749/50; another entry in the parish register indicated Emanuel Mallance and Margaret Reeves married 11 Feb 1750)

Reeves, Tabitha and James Graves married 26 Jul 1764 (her name was listed as Tab. Reevs in the parish register)

Renaud, John, see "Aranea Slemaker," q.v.

Renner, Catherine and George Spear, both of Baltimore County, married 24 May 1795 (her name was mistakenly listed as Birmer in my 1987 book; they were married by virtue of the publication of banns)

Renshaw, Joseph and Elizabeth Wells married 28 Oct 1742 (his name was misspelled Reneher in my 1987 book)

Renshaw, Martin (of Baltimore County) and Magdaline Jones (of Harford County) married 19 Nov 1788 (her first name was listed as Madgalen in my 1987 book)

Rhodes, Abraham and Roxanna Standiford married 6 Aug 1772 (her name was listed as Roxa. in the parish register)

Rhodes, Frances and John Nelson married 15 Nov 1715 (her last name was not indicated in the parish register, but *Baltimore County Families, 1659-1759* indicated John Nelson and Frances Rhodes married 12 Jan 1718; his name was listed as Nellson in my 1987 book and the parish register was difficult to read, but the date was clearly 15 Nov 1715)

Rhodes, John and Sarah Standiford married 25 -- 1768 (probably married 25 Oct 1768, but the information was incomplete in the parish register)

Rhodes, Magdelen, see "Rebecca Rhodes," q.v.

Rhodes, Rebecca, daughter of Richard and Magdelen, born 20 Mar 1723 (her first name was misspelled Rebeca in my 1987 book)

Rhodes, Richard and Susan Prosper married 16 Apr 1769 (his name was listed as Rodes in the parish register)

Rhodes, Richard, see "Rebecca Rhodes," q.v.

Rhodous, Joseph and Ann Polson married -- Jun 1725 (their names were listed as shown in my 1987 book, but her name was listed as Polion in *Maryland Marriages, 1634-1777*)

Rice, Hannah, see "Hannah Ruse," q.v.

Rice, Mary and Edward Manby or Manley married 30 Aug 1761 (his name is difficult to read in the parish register and it could have been Manby or Manley)

Richardson, Ann and John Roberts married 6 Feb 1714 (her name was listed as Richarson in my 1987 book)

Richardson, James and Rachael Stone or Stones married 16 Jan 1758 (her name was difficult to read in the parish register and it could have been Stone, Stones or even Stokes)

Richardson, Letitia and Adam McClung married 24 Dec 1764 (his name was listed as M'Clong in the parish register)

Richardson, Thomas and Sarah Standiford married 20 May 1720 (although her name was listed as Standove in the parish register and in my 1987 book, it was listed as Standifor in *Maryland Marriages, 1634-1777*)

Ricketts, Benjamin and Mary Cutchin married 2 Jun 1759 (this marriage was entered in the parish register among the 1758 marriages)

Rider, Mary and Joseph Jennings married 23 May 1743 (his name was mistakenly listed as Lennings and Jenings in my 1987 book and the year of marriage was mistakenly listed as 1742; another entry in the parish register indicated they married 24 Apr 1743; the earlier date could have been their intention of marriage or publication of banns)

Rigbie, Ann and Luke Raven married 20 Aug 1765 (his name was listed a Reaven in the parish register)

Rigbie, Rachael and John Willion married 10 Nov 1763 (his name was difficult to read in the parish register and it could have been Jno. Willion or Jno. Willson; her name was listed as Rigbee)

Rigdon, Ann and Daniel Preston married 28 May 1772 (his name was mistakenly listed as Dreston in my 1987 book)

Right, William, see "William Wright," q.v.

Riset, Rachel and James Pring married in 1753 (the complete date was not given in the parish register)

Risteau, Mary, see "Mary Ristone," q.v.

Ristien, Thomas and Margret Sinkler married 28 Nov 1751 (another entry in the parish register indicated Thomas Ryston and Margaret Sinclair married subsequent to November, 1751, but the exact date was not given)

Ristone, Abraham and Elianor Farlow or Harlow married 11 Nov 1762 (her name was difficult to read in the parish register)

Ristone, John and Sarah Sinclair or Sinkler married 17 May 1747 (another entry in the parish register indicated they married 21 May 1747)

Ristone, Mary and Isaac Sampson married 17 Apr 1747 (another entry in the parish register indicated Isaac Samson and Mary Risteau married 20 Apr 1747)

Roach, William and Elizabeth Hambleton, both of Harford County, married 27 Jan 1793 (they were married by virtue of the publication of banns)

Robell(?), Robert and Elizabeth Bradfield married 23 Mar 1746 (the date should actually be written 23 Mar 1746/7; another entry in the parish register indicated Robert Cabell and Elizabeth Bradfield married 3 Nov 1746; the earlier date could have been their intention of marriage or publication of banns)

Robenson, Richard Jr. and Jemima Robertson married 15 Sep 1748 (this marriage was entered in the parish register among the 1748 marriages and another entry in the parish register indicated they married subsequent to 4 Sep 1748, but the exact date was not given; the marriage date was mistakenly listed as 15 Sep 1749 in my 1987 book)

Roberts, Ann and Joseph Sadlers married 11 -- 1768 (probably married 11 Oct 1768, but the information was incomplete in the parish register)

Roberts, Ashell and Mary Ingrim married 16 Dec 1742 (his name was misspelled Asraell in my 1987 book; another entry in the parish register indicated Asahell Roberts and Mary Ingram married 5 Dec 1742; the earlier date could have been their intention of marriage or publication of banns)

Roberts, John and Ann Richardson married 6 Feb 1714 (her name was listed as Richarson in my 1987 book)

Roberts, John Peter and Maria Sanderson, both of Harford County, married 23 Apr 1792 (the parish register indicated they were married by virtue of a license from Harford County, but no marriage license was found in Harford or Baltimore County)

Robertson, Edward and Margaret Standiford married 21 Apr 1752 (her name was listed as Standeford in my 1987 book)

Robertson, Jemima and Richard Robenson, Jr. married 15 Sep 1748 (this marriage was entered in the parish register among the 1748 marriages and another entry in the parish register indicated they married subsequent to 4 Sep 1748, but the exact date was not given; the marriage date was mistakenly listed as 15 Sep 1749 in my 1987 book)

Robertson, Jemima and John Standiford married 11 Jan 1759 (his name was listed as Standeford in my 1987 book)

Robertson, Robert and Sarah Taylor married 9 Nov 1721 (his name was listed as Roberson in my 1987 book)

Robertson, Susannah and William Frost married 21 Dec 1749 (another entry in the parish register indicated they married subsequent to 17 Dec 1749, but the exact date was not given, and her last name was listed as Roberson; Susannah was mistakenly listed as Suhannah in my 1987 book)

Robeson, James and Ann Asher married 7 Jun 1752 (her name was listed as Ashor in my 1987 book)

Robinson, Charles, see "Walter Robinson," q.v.

Robinson, Elizabeth and James Isham or Ishum married ---- (no date was given in the parish register, but it was listed among the 1717-1718 marriages; his name was mistakenly listed as Jeames Isinn (Lsinn) in my 1987 book; James Isham or Ishum married Elizabeth Robinson, admx. of William Robinson, by June 1719, as noted in *Baltimore County Families, 1659-1759*)

Robinson, Mepthlika, see "Walter Robinson," q.v.

Robinson, Walter, born 24 May 1790, son of Charles and Mepthlika or Lytica (although his mother's name appeared only as the initial "M" in my 1987 book, it looked like Mepthlika in another part of the parish register; she was probably the Miss Lytica Galloway who married Charles Robinson on 29 Jun 1787 in Baltimore County as cited in *Maryland Marriages, 1778-1800*)

Rock, Rachael and James Clarke married 28 May 1769 (the exact date was not given, but their request to publish marriage banns was entered in the parish register and their names were listed as James Clark and Rachel Rock at that time)

Rock, Thomas and Rebecca Reed, both of Harford County, married 29 May 1791 (they were married by virtue of the publication of banns)

Rockhold, Asael and Ann Roe married 3 Apr 1749 (another entry in the parish register indicated "Asall Rockhold and Anne Row this court married" subsequent to 26 Mar 1749, but the exact date was not given)

Rockhold, Asel and Mary Rutledge married circa 1771? (the exact date of marriage was not given, but their request to publish marriage banns was entered in the parish register among others dated 1766, 1771, and 1775)

Rockhold, Elizabeth and Jacob Standiford married 29 -- 1768 (probably married 29 Sep 1768, but the information was incomplete in the parish register)

Rockhold, John and Jemima Deason married 14 Jul 1771 (her name was listed as Deeson in the parish register)

Rockhold, John and Martha Waters, both of Harford County, married 2 Feb 1790 (his name looked like Rockhold or Borkhold in different parts of the parish register, but it was listed as Rockhold in *Maryland Marriages, 1778-1800*)

Rockhold, Ruth and John Williams married 17 Apr 1749 (another entry in the parish register indicated they married some time between 26 Mar and 14 May 1749, but the exact date was not given)

Roe (Row), Ann(e) and Asael Rockhold married 3 Apr 1749 (another entry in the parish register indicated "Asall Rockhold and Anne Row this court married" subsequent to 26 Mar 1749, but the exact date was not given)

Roe (Row), Mary and Benjamin Rutledge married 28 Apr 1748 (another entry in the parish register indicated they married 3 Apr 1748; the earlier date could have been their intention of marriage or publication of banns)

Rogers, Dorothy and John Harris married -- Dec 1721 (the day of marriage was not indicated in the parish register and his name was mistakenly listed as James Harris in *Maryland Marriages, 1634-1777*)

Rogers, John and Rebecca Stevens married 25 Apr 1714 (their names had were listed as John Roggers and Receckah Stevens in my 1987 book)

Rollo, Archibald, son of Archibald and Rebecca, born 11 Jan 1716 (his name was listed as Archiball Rollar, son of Archeball and Rebekaha, in my 1987 book)

Rooke, Thomas and Mary Flannagan married 6 Nov 1770 (her name was listed as Flanngin in my 1987 book)

Roose, James and Margret Kitely married 22 Mar 1773 (her name was mistakenly listed as Hitely in my 1987 book)

Row, John and Deborah Jones married 17 Dec 1761 (her name was listed as Deb. in the parish register)

Rowing, John and Comfort Brown married 14 Feb 1751 (another entry in the parish register indicated they married in 1751, but the exact date was not given, and his name was listed as Rownes)

Rozomister, Cathrine and Michael Clebedints married 27 Mar 1763 (her name was difficult to read in the parish register and it was listed as Cath. Roza Mister or Cath. Rozamister since Cath. Roza was written on one line and mister was written on the next line, but with no hyphen in between)

Ruff, Daniel and Hannah Moffett married 31 Dec 1801 (they were married by virtue of a license issued on 8 Dec 1801; her name was listed as Maffitt in another part of the parish register and in my 1987 book)

Rumsey, Benjamin (of Cecil County, attorney at law) and Mary Hall (daughter of Col. John Hall of Baltimore County) married 24 Mar 1768 (the year of marriage was omitted from my 1987 book)

Rumsey, Charlotte (of Harford County) and Edward Aquila Howard, Edward Aquila (of Baltimore) married 11 Dec 1798 (they were married by virtue of a license issued on 10 Dec 1798)

Ruse (Rice?), Hannah and Morgan Conway married 12 Aug 1761 (her name was difficult to read in the parish register and it could have been Ruse, Rise or Rice)

Rush, Arnold and Jane or Janett Conn, both of Harford County, married 27 Aug 1792 (the parish register indicated they were married by virtue of a license issued in Harford County on 25 Aug 1792, but no marriage license was found in Harford or Baltimore County; it is interesting to note that there was a marriage between Arnold Rush and Esther Conn in Harford County, but it was not until 1813)

Ruth, Jacob and Sarah Airs married 2 Sep 1759 (their marriage date was mistakenly entered as 2 Apr 1759 in my 1987 book)

Rutledge, Benjamin and Mary Roe or Row married 28 Apr 1748 (another entry in the parish register indicated they married 3 Apr 1748; the earlier date could have been their intention of marriage or publication of banns)

Rutledge, Elizabeth and Benjamin Jerman married 28 Nov 1753 (another entry in the parish register indicated they married in 1753, but the exact date was not given; his name was listed as Terman or Jerman in my 1987 book)

Rutledge, Ephraim and Susan Pocock married 6 Feb 1766 (his name was listed as Eprmarried and her name was listed as Poccock in the parish register)

Rutledge, Hannah and William Jennings married 20 Aug 1770 (her name was listed as Rutlidge in my 1987 book)

Rutledge, John and Ruth Standiford married 4 Feb 1773 (his name was listed as Rutlidge in the parish register)

Rutledge, Kezia and John Parks married 3 Nov 1761 (her name was mistakenly listed as Lezia in my 1987 book)

Rutledge, Mary and Asel Rockhold married circa 1771? (the exact date of marriage was not given, but their request to publish marriage banns was entered in the parish register among several others dated 1766, 1771 and 1775)

Rutledge, Ruth and John Standiford married 15 Dec 1771 (her name was listed as Ruthe Rutlidge in the parish register)

Rutledge, Sophia and Nathaniel Wright married 11 Apr 1769 (her name was listed as Rutlege in the parish register)

Ryan, Peter and Mary Symson married 21 Dec 1749 (his name was listed as Ryon in my 1987 book)

Ryley, Mary and Edward McCullister married 21 Oct 1754 (his name was listed his name as M'Cullister in the parish register)

Rynoo, Mary and William Williams married 6 -- 1768 (probably married 6 Oct 1768, but the information was incomplete in the parish register)

Sadler, Thomas and Elizabeth Howard, both of Baltimore County, married 7 Nov 1793 (they were married by virtue of a license issued on 6 Nov 1793 and it listed her name as Eliza G. Howard)

Sadlers, Joseph and Ann Roberts married 11 -- 1768 (probably married 11 Oct 1768, but the information was incomplete in the parish register)

Sampson, Isaac and Mary Ristone married 17 Apr 1747 (another entry in the parish register indicated Isaac Samson and Mary Risteau married 20 Apr 1747)

Samson, Benjamin and Jemima Standiford married 11 Feb 1766 (her name was mistakenly listed as Jemoma Standeford in my 1987 book)

Sandage, John and Sarah Grover married 19 Sep 1751 (another entry in the parish register indicated they married 25 Aug 1751 and his name was listed as Sandige; the earlier date could have been their intention of marriage or publication of banns)

Sanders, Charity and Benjamin Vanhorn, both of Harford County, married 15 Feb 1791 (they were married by virtue of the publication of banns)

Sanderson, Maria and John Peter Roberts, both of Harford County, married 23 Apr 1792 (the parish register indicated they were married by virtue of a license from Harford County, but no marriage license was found in Harford or Baltimore County)

Saunders, Robert and Elizabeth Andrew married 28 Apr 1765 (her name in the parish register could be either Eliz. Andrew or Andrews)

Scarborough, Mary and John Moore, both of Harford County, married 3 Aug 1797 (her name was listed as Scarborough in the parish register; a marriage license was issued on 3 Aug 1797 and listed her name as Scarbrough)

Scarf, Amelia and Benjamin Guyton married 13 Dec 1753 (his name was mistakenly listed as Giyton in my 1987 book)

Scharf, Elizabeth and Peter Skarabon married 13 Mar 1745 (the spelling of his name is unclear in the parish register)

Scimmons, Charles and Elizabeth Poteet married 19 Oct 1742 (another entry in the parish register listed their names as Charles Scimmons and Elizabeth Poteett; his name was mistakenly listed as Summons in my 1987 book and her name was misspelled Pottet; *Maryland Marriages, 1634-1777* listed his name as Simmons)

Scimmons, Thomas and Priscilla McComas married 6 Feb 1753 (her name was listed as Pricilla Maccomas in the parish register)

Scotland, William and Elizabeth Taylor married 13 Jul 1749 (another entry in the parish register indicated William Scott and Elizabeth Taylor married 2 Jul 1749; it is possible that "Scott and" could have been transcribed as "Scotland" and since they are listed as two separate marriages in *Maryland Marriages, 1634-1777*, this remains unclear)

Scott, Abarillah and John Durbin married 20 Aug 1715 (their names were listed as John Derbin and Abrillah Scott in my 1987 book)

Scott, Daniel and Margaret Short, both of Harford County, married 6 Apr 1797 (they were married by virtue of a license issued that same day)

Scott, Elizabeth and William McComas married 22 Jan 1760 (his name was listed as Maccomus in the parish register)

Scott, Elizabeth and Daniel McComas, both of Harford County, married 18 Feb 1796 (they were married by virtue of a license issued that same day)

Scott, James and Mary Martin married 12 Nov 1749 (another entry in the parish register indicated they married some time between 24 Sep and 26 Nov 1749, but the exact date was not given)

Scott, James and Cassandra Bond married 15 Apr 1770 (her name was listed as Casandera in the parish register)

Scott, Jean, see "Jane Watson," q.v.

Scott, Joseph Jr. (of Baltimore County) and Hannah Norris (of Harford County) married 5 Mar 1795 (his name was inadvertently listed without the Jr. in my 1987 book; they were married by virtue of a license issued in Baltimore County on 4 Mar 1795)

Scott, William, see "William Scotland," q.v.

Scotter, Devans and Mary Forrord married 9 Jul 1761 (her name was difficult to read in the parish register and it could have been Forrord or Porrord)

Seemons, Hannah and Thomas Hutchens married 12 May 1736 (her name was misspelled Seemmons in my 1987 book)

Shadows, David and Ann Boswell married 26 Dec 1749 (another entry in the parish register indicated they married subsequent to 17 Dec 1749, but the exact date was not given, and her name was listed as Anne Bozwell)

Shafford, Robert and Catherine ---- married 17 -- 1768 (probably married 17 Sep 1768, but the information was incomplete in the parish register)

Shannom, Elizabeth and Benjamin Gaton married 26 Oct 1750 (her name was mistakenly listed as Skinnoni in my 1987 book)

Shannom, Thomas and Elizabeth Kersey married 26 Sep 1750 (his name was listed as Shannern in my 1987 book and as Shannem in *Maryland Marriages, 1634-1777*)

Sharpe, Horatio, see "John Mercer," q.v.

Shaw, Daniel and Prudence Bosley married 14 Apr 1763 (her name was listed as Bozley in the parish register)

Shaw, Frances and Thomas Morris married 10 Oct 1749 (another entry in the parish register indicated they married some time between 24 Sep and 26 Nov 1749, but the exact date was not given)

Shaw, Sarah and Simon Person married 2 Feb 1715 (her name was spelled Schaw and his name was listed as Symon Person and Simon Pearson at various times in the parish register and in my 1987 book)

Shaw, Susannah and John Kersey, Jr. married 27 Feb 1749 (the date should actually be written 27 Feb 1749/50; her name was mistakenly listed as Suhannah in my 1987 book)

Shaw, Weymouth and Ann Worthington married 23 Apr 1761 (his name was listed as Weymoth in the parish register)

Shelly, Susannah and Edward Read married in 1771 (the exact date of marriage was not given, but their request to publish marriage banns was entered in the parish register on 15 Sep 1771)

Shepard, Mary and Joseph Smith married 15 Oct 1747 (another entry in the parish register indicated they married 5 Jul 1747; the earlier date could have been their intention of marriage or publication of banns)

Shepard, Tarrisha and Benjamin Deason married 9 Dec 1742 (another entry in the parish register indicated Benjamin Deason and ---- Shepard, both of this parish, married 21 Nov 1742; the earlier date could have been their intention of marriage or publication of banns)

Shepperd, Jenitia, daughter of William and Margaret, born 2 Oct 1726 (her name was listed as Lenitia Sheppard in my 1987 book and as Jenitia Shepperd in *Baltimore County Families, 1659-1759*)

Sheredine, Mary and William Neill, both of Harford County, married 2 Nov 1797 (they were married by virtue of a license issued on that same day)

Sheredine, Thomas and Ann Neill, both of Harford County, married 9 Mar 1797 (they were married by virtue of a license issued on 19 Mar 1797; her name listed as Neil in the parish register)

Sherelock, John and Elizabeth Cheshire married 30 Nov 1737 (her name was listed as Chesher in my 1987 book)

Shoebridge, John and Mary Norris married 28 Oct 1732 (the date of marriage was mistakenly listed as 28 Sep 1732 and her surname was misspelled as Morris in my 1987 book; his name was listed as Shewbridge in other parts of the parish register)

Short, Margaret and Daniel Scott, both of Harford County, married 6 Apr 1797 (they were married by virtue of a license issued that same day)

Shoudy, Francis and Louranna Taylor married 13 Sep 1754 (their names were listed as Francis Showdy and Louzanna Taylor in my 1987 book and

Maryland Marriages, 1634-1777; she may have been Lurene Taylor, born 1733, daughter of James Taylor)

Shoudy, Rachel and Thomas Durham, both of Harford County, married 20 Feb 1791 (they were married by virtue of the publication of banns; her name was listed as Shondy or Shoudy in my 1987 book and the marriage date was mistakenly listed as 15 Mar 1791; his name was listed as Dunham in another part of the parish register)

Sickelmore, Ruth Sarah, daughter of Samuel and Ruth, born 23 Dec 1715 (her name was listed as Ruth Saray Sickemore, daughter of Samevell Sickemore and Ruth, in my 1987 book)

Sickelmore, Samuel and Katherine Herrington married 12 Sep 1716 (their names were listed as Samevall Scickemore and Katerne Herrington in the parish register and in my 1987 book)

Sickelmore, Sutton and Prudence Hendon married 29 Jul 1762 (their names were listed as Sicklemore and Hindon in my 1987 book)

Simkins, Margaret and Charles Prosser married 27 Sep 1753 (another entry in the parish register indicated they married in 1753, but the exact date was not given and her name was listed as Margrett Synkins)

Simmons, George and Jemima Standiford married 7 Dec 1736 (his name was mistakenly listed as Summons in my 1987 book and her name was listed as Standeford)

Simmons, Mary and Jonathan Starkey married 23 Jun 1757 (their marriage date was mistakenly listed as 30 Jun in my 1987 book)

Simmons, Rachel and Luke Pendergest married 26 Jan 1768 (his name was mistakenly listed as Luke Pinder Gist in my 1987 book)

Simpson, Elizabeth, see "Elizabeth Sympson" and "John Cox," q.v.

Sinkler, James and Jane Macmar married 1 Dec 1767 (their names were listed as Jas. Sinkler and Jane McMar in *Maryland Marriages, 1634-1777*)

Sinkler, Margret and Thomas Ristien married 28 Nov 1751 (another entry in the parish register indicated Thomas Ryston and Margaret Sinclair married subsequent to November, 1751, but the exact date was not given)

Sinkler, Sarah and John Ristone married 17 May 1747 (another entry in the parish register indicated they married 21 May 1747 and spelled her name Sinclair)

Skarabon, Peter and Elizabeth Scharf married 13 Mar 1745 (the spelling of his last name is unclear in the parish register)

Skipper (Skippen?), James and Ann Wareing or Warring married 10 Nov 1753 (another entry in the parish register indicated James Skipen and Anne Warring married in 1753, but the exact date was not given)

Slater, John and Roannah or Rosannah Pollard married 18 Aug 1755 (her name was difficult to read in the parish register and it could have been Roannah or Rosannah)

Slemaker, Aranea and Henry Patrick Finnagan, both of Harford County, married 26 Apr 1792 (her name was mistakenly listed as Aransa Demaker in my 1987 book and the marriage date was mistakenly listed as 17 Jun 1792; they were married by virtue of a license issued on 25 Apr 1792 which listed their

names as H. Patrick Finnagan and Areanea Slemaker; there was a subsequent
license for Ariana Finagan and John Renaud issued on 25 Aug 1796 in
Harford County)

Slowin, John and Elizabeth Smith married 17 Oct 1770 (her name was listed as
Eliz. in the parish register)

Smart family names (references to this family were indicated in the index of my
1987 book, but they are not in said book nor are they in Reamy's *St.
George's Parish Register, 1689-1793*; since the surname index to my book
was prepared long ago by Lucy Harrison, it cannot now be determined how
the discrepancy arose)

Smith, Catherine and James Baker married 25 Sep 1742 (her name was
misspelled Cathrene in my 1987 book)

Smith, Elizabeth and John Slowin married 17 Oct 1770 (her name was listed as
Eliz. in the parish register)

Smith, Henry and Elizabeth Druley married -- Jun 1738 (this same information
was listed in *Maryland Marriages, 1634-1777* which also indicated Henry
Smith and Eliz. Dury married 6 Jun 1738 in Talbot County)

Smith, Isabella and Andrew Stevenson, both of Harford County, married 30 Nov
1793 (the parish register indicated they were married by virtue of a license
issued in Harford County, but no marriage license was found in Harford or
Baltimore County)

Smith, James and Sarah Haley, both of Harford County, married 20 Sep 1797
(the marriage date was mistakenly listed as 21 Sep 1797 in my 1987 book;
they were issued a marriage license on 20 Sep 1797 and married the same
day)

Smith, Joseph and Mary Shepard married 15 Oct 1747 (another entry in the
parish register indicated they married 5 Jul 1747; the earlier date could have
been their intention of marriage or publication of banns)

Smith, Lambert and Elizabeth Gittings, both of Baltimore County, married 6
Nov 1792 (they were married by virtue of a license issued on 3 Nov 1792)

Smith, Mary and Edmond Hays married -- Nov 1731 (his first name was listed
as Edmond in my 1987 book and as Edmund in *Baltimore County Families,
1659-1759*, but this marriage was not listed in *Maryland Marriages, 1634-
1777*)

Smith, Mary and John Chennerworth married 26 Nov 1730 (the more common
spellings of his name was Chenowith and Chinworth; although the date of
marriage was entered in the parish register as 26 Nov 1730/31 this is
incorrect because "double dating" applied only to dates from 1 Jan to 24 Mar
in the old style calendar)

Smith, Rachel, see "William Smith," q.v.

Smith, Samuel and Jane Parrish married 31 Dec 1743 (another entry in the
parish register indicated they married 18 Dec 1743 and her name was listed
as Jean Parish; the earlier date could have been their intention of marriage or
publication of banns)

Smith, William, son of William and Rachel, born 28 Oct 1722 (no date of birth was given in my 1987 book, but it was noted in *Baltimore County Families, 1659-1759*)

Smith, William and Anne Peacock married -- Dec 1751 (the complete date was not given in the parish register)

Smith, William and Rebecca Wheeler married 26 Nov 1772 (her name was listed as Whelar in the parish register)

Smith, William and ---- married 17 -- 1768 (probably married 17 Sep 1768, but the information was incomplete in the parish register)

Smithson, Ann, see "Avarilla Smithson," q.v.

Smithson, Avarilla, daughter of Thomas and Ann, born 28 Dec 1720 (the year of birth was omitted from my 1987 book)

Smithson, Eleanor and Samuel Durham married 15 Jan 1723 (they were listed as Samuel Durram and Elinor Smithson married 15 Jan 17-- in my 1987 book)

Smithson, Elizabeth and Henry Dorsey (son of Edward), both of Harford County, married 5 Feb 1795 (they were married by virtue of a license issued in Harford County on that same day)

Smithson, Ruth and Basil Billingsley married 29 Jan 1767 (his name was listed as Bazl. in the parish register)

Smithson, Thomas, see "Avarilla Smithson," q.v.

Sparks, Sarah and Philip Lock Elliott married 3 Sep 1762 (his name was listed as Phill. Lock Elliott in the parish register and mistakenly listed as Phill. Lock Ellcott in my 1987 book and in *Maryland Marriages, 1634-1777*; his correct full name was Philip Lock Elliott as noted in William Wright's admin. account in 1750)

Spear, George and Catherine Renner, both of Baltimore County, married 24 May 1795 (her name was mistakenly listed as Birmer in my 1987 book; they were married by virtue of the publication of banns)

Spencer, Hannah and John Burnet, both of Harford County, married 28 Nov 1788 (his name was listed as Burnett and their marriage date was mistakenly listed as 23 Nov 1788 in my 1987 book)

Standiford, Abraham and Susan Chamberlaine married 8 Oct 1769 (her name was mistakenly listed as Chaberlane in my 1987 book)

Standiford, Aquila and Sarah Clark married 27 Dec 1764 (his name was listed as Aqa. Standeford in the parish register)

Standiford, Archibald and Elizabeth Armstrong married 25 Jun 1754 (his name was listed as Archd. Standeford in the parish register and their marriage was entered among the 1756 marriages)

Standiford, Avarilla and John James married 14 Apr 1761 (her name was listed as Standeford in my 1987 book)

Standiford, Cloe and Willliam Edey married 22 Nov 1770 (his name was listed as Edye in my 1987 book)

Standiford, Edmond and Hannah Gray, both of Harford County, married 13 Oct 1787 (his first name was listed as Edmund in my 1987 book)

Standiford, Israel, son of John and Margrett, born 4 Sep 1720 (his name was listed as Israell Standafar in my 1987 book)

Standiford, Israel and Cassandra Anderson married 6 Jan 1743 (the date should actually be written 6 Jan 1743/4; his name was listed as Standeford in my 1987 book)

Standiford, Jacob and Elizabeth Rockhold married 29 -- 1768 (probably married 29 Sep 1768, but the information was incomplete in the parish register)

Standiford, Jemima and George Simmons married 7 Dec 1736 (his name was mistakenly listed as Summons in my 1987 book and her name was listed as Standeford)

Standiford, Jemima and Marberril Elliott married 13 Jan 1756 (their names were listed in the parish register as "Marberril, Elliott & Jemima Standeford")

Standiford, Jemima and Benjamin Samson married 11 Feb 1766 (her name was mistakenly listed as Jemoma Standeford in my 1987 book)

Standiford, John, see "Israel Standiford," q.v.

Standiford, John and Jemima Robertson married 11 Jan 1759 (his name was listed as Standeford in my 1987 book)

Standiford, John and Ruth Rutledge married 15 Dec 1771 (her name was listed as Ruthe Rutlidge in the parish register)

Standiford, Margaret and Edward Robertson married 21 Apr 1752 (her name was listed as Standeford in my 1987 book)

Standiford, Margrett, see "Israel Standiford," q.v.

Standiford, Mary and Nicholas Hutchins, Jr. married 4 Jan 1763 (her name was listed as Standeford in my 1987 book)

Standiford, Mary and Jacob Marshall married 5 Jun 1774 (her name was listed as Sandeford and his name as Marshal in my 1987 book)

Standiford, Mary, see "Jacob Sandiford," q.v.

Standiford, Phillisanna and Richard Hutchens married 20 Jan 1767 (her name was listed as Philliszaner Standeford in the parish register)

Standiford, Roxanna and Abraham Rhodes married 6 Aug 1772 (her name was listed as Roxa. in the parish register)

Standiford, Ruth and John Rutledge married 4 Feb 1773 (his name was listed as Rutlidge in the parish register)

Standiford, Sarah and Thomas Richardson married 20 May 1720 (although her name was listed as Standove in the parish register and in my 1987 book, it was listed as Standifor in *Maryland Marriages, 1634-1777*)

Standiford, Sarah and John Rhodes married 25 -- 1768 (probably married 25 Oct 1768, but the information was incomplete in the parish register)

Standiford, Skelton Jr. and Elizabeth Pocock married 4 Nov 1755 (her name was listed as Eliz. in the parish register and his as Standeford in the my 1987 book)

Standiford, William and Elizabeth Carlile married 16 Jul 1750 (her name was listed as Eliz. in the parish register and his name was listed as Standeford in my 1987 book)

Standiford, William Jr. and Rebecca Deason married 27 May 1767 (her name was listed as Reb. in the parish register and his name was listed as Wm. Standeford Jnr.)

Stansbury, Hannah and Richard Coop married 10 Dec 1747 (another entry in the parish register indicated they married 6 Dec 1747 and his name was listed as Coup)

Stansbury, Rachel and Alexius Lemmon married 29 Nov 1771 (his name was strangely listed as Eliz'th Leemon in the parish register)

Stansbury, Rebeckah and Thomas Bond married 19 Dec 1771 (her name was mistakenly listed as Reneckah in my 1987 book)

Stansbury, Richardson and Mary Raven married 23 Feb 1747 (her name was listed as Reaven in the parish register)

Stansbury, Susanna and William Wilkinson Waits, both of Baltimore County, married 4 Dec 1792 (they were married by virtue of a license issued on 7 Nov 1792 and listed his name as Waits and spelled her name Susannah; *Baltimore County Marriage Licenses, 1777-1798* mistakenly listed his name as Wails)

Stansbury, Tabitha and William Hicks married 24 Dec 1747 (another entry in the parish register indicated they married some time between 6 Dec 1747 and 3 Jan 1748, but the exact date was not given)

Starkey, Hannah and Joss. or Josh. Hindon married 9 Jan 1766 (his name was difficult to read in the parish register, but it could be Joss. with an elevated "s" or Josh. with an elevated "h" and his last name was either Hindon or Hendon)

Starkey, Jonathan and Mary Simmons married 23 Jun 1757 (their marriage date was mistakenly listed as 30 Jun in my 1987 book)

Steadman, James and Mary Minson married 10 Oct 1747 (her name was mistakenly listed as Munson in my 1987 book; *Maryland Marriages, 1634-1777* has listed both marriage dates and listed her name once as Misnon, an apparent typographical error; another entry in the parish register indicated James Steedman and Mary Minson married 23 Aug 1747; the earlier date could have been their intention of marriage or publication of banns)

Steel, James and Elizabeth Tomley married 3 Feb 1743 (the date should actually be written 3 Feb 1743/4; another entry in the parish register indicated they married 29 Jan 1744 and her name was listed as Tomlin; her name was listed as Tornley or Tomley in my 1987 book)

Stephens, Mary, see "William Cole" and "Mary Stevens," q.v.

Stevens, Ann(e) and John Campbell married 7 Apr 1751 (the exact date was not given in my 1987 book; his name was listed as Cammell in the parish register)

Stevens, Ephraim and Temperance Green married 28 Jan 1768 (his name was listed as Eprmarried in the parish register)

Stevens, Martha and William Reaves married in summer of 1742 (her name was actually entered as "Martha Stevens Quart." in the parish register)

Stevens, Mary and William Cole married 21 Nov 1742 (another entry in the parish register listed her name as Stephens and their marriage date as 16 Nov 1742; the earlier date could have been their intention of marriage or publication of banns)

Stevens, Rebecca and John Rogers married 25 Apr 1714 (their names had were listed as John Roggers and Receckah Stevens in my 1987 book)

Stevens, Samuel and ---- married Shrove Tuesday, 1723 (information was incomplete in the parish register; this marriage was inadvertently omitted from *Maryland Marriages, 1634-1777*)

Stevenson, Andrew and Isabella Smith, both of Harford County, married 30 Nov 1793 (the parish register indicated they were married by virtue of a license issued in Harford County, but no marriage license was found in Harford or Baltimore County)

Stevenson, John and Anther or Auther Wyle married 11 Aug 1763 (her first name appeared somewhat unusual in spelling, so perhaps she could have been Athea Wyle, daughter of Luke Wyle)

Stevenson, Jonas and Rachel Hughes married 12 May 1799 (they were married by virtue of a license issued on 10 May 1799)

Stevert (Stovert?), Alexander and Mary McKinley married 11 Dec 1754 (her name was listed as M'Kinley in the parish register)

Steward, Elizabeth, see "Elizabeth Stewart," q.v.

Stewart, Cornelius and Mary Low married 25 Nov 1747 (his first name was misspelled Cornelias in my 1987 book; another entry in the parish register indicated Cornelius Steward and Mary Lowe married in 1747, but the exact date was not given)

Stewart, Elizabeth and John Poulson married 8 Apr 1750 (another entry in the parish register indicated John Boulson and Elizabeth Steward married in 1750, but the exact date was not given)

Stiles, Elizabeth and John Emes married -- Sep 1749 (the exact date was not given, but it was apparently some time between 3 Sep and 24 Sep 1749)

Stocksdale, Thomas and Sarah Baxter, both of Harford County, married 18 Dec 1797 (they were married by virtue of a license issued on that same day)

Stokes, Rachael, see "Rachael Stone (Stones)," q.v.

Stolinger, George and Ann Deaver married 23 Jan 1800 (her name was mistakenly listed as Doover in my 1987 book)

Stone (Stones), Rachael and James Richardson married 16 Jan 1758 (her name was difficult to read in the parish register and it could have been Stone, Stones or even Stokes)

Strickland, John and Alice Perry, both of Harford County, married 30 Jun 1793 (they were married by virtue of the publication of banns)

Sullivan, John and Kitty Groves married 25 Dec 1771 (their names were listed as John Soullavin and Kitty Grooves in the parish register)

Sunk, George and Elizabeth Pennington married 23 Sep 1766 (this entry in the parish register was actually listed as "Geo. Sunk & Eliz. Pennenton, Eliz. Pennington marrd. Sep 23d 1766")

Sutton, Jane and Philip Hodge married 13 Mar 1774 (her name was listed as Sutten in my 1987 book)

Sutton, Ruth and Addam Hance married 25 Oct 1744 (another entry in the parish register indicated Adam Hendress and Ruth Sutton married subsequent to 23 Sep 1744, but the exact date was not given)

Swan, Dorothy and William Demmett (son of William) married 14 Dec 1765
(another entry in the parish register indicated William Demmett and Dorthy
Swan married 13 Dec 1765; information in my 1987 book was incorrect in
that it mistakenly stated William Demmett, son of William Demmett and
Dorothy Swan, was born 14 Dec 1765)

Swarth (Swarts), Sarah and Kidd Lynch, both of Harford County, married 21
Aug 1791 (her name was mistakenly listed as Sumarts in my 1987 book and
as Swasth or Swarth in another part of the parish register; they were married
by virtue of the publication of banns)

Swift, Mark and Ann Lockerd married 26 Dec 1725 (although her name was
misspelled Lockeord and the date of marriage was listed as 2- Dec 1725 in
my 1987 book, it was noted as Lockerd and dated 26 Dec 1725 in *Maryland
Marriages, 1634-1777*)

Swinard, John and Sarah Wilson or Willson married 30 Apr 1747 (his name was
mistakenly listed as Surnard in my 1987 book; another entry in the parish
register indicated they married 12 Apr 1747; the earlier date could have been
their intention of marriage or publication of banns)

Sympson, Elizabeth and John Cox married 30 Nov 1742 (her name was listed as
Eliz. Simpson in *Maryland Marriages, 1634-1777*)

Symson, Mary and Peter Ryan married 21 Dec 1749 (his name was listed as
Ryon in my 1987 book)

Synkins, Margrett, see "Margaret Simkins," q.v.

Talbott, Vincent and Elizabeth Bosley married 2 Feb 1773 (her name was listed
as Bozley in my 1987 book)

Tapper, Mary, see "Mary Tipper," q.v.

Tate, Bridget, see "Brigitt Teate," q.v.

Taylor, Abraham and Dinah or Dinna White married 20 -- 1708? (their date of
marriage was incomplete in the parish register and even though it was listed
among the marriages and births circa 1713-1714, their first child Robert was
born 13 Oct 1709 as noted in *Baltimore County Families, 1659-1759*)

Taylor, Abraham, see "Robert Taylor," q.v.

Taylor, Charlotte and Ephraim Donovan, both of Harford County, married 28
Mar 1791 (his name was listed as Donavon in the parish register)

Taylor, Dinah, see "Robert Taylor," q.v.

Taylor, Elizabeth and William Scotland married 13 Jul 1749 (another entry in
the parish register indicated William Scott and Elizabeth Taylor married 2
Jul 1749; it is possible that "Scott and" could have been transcribed as
"Scotland" and since they are listed as two separate marriages in *Maryland
Marriages, 1634-1777*, this remains unclear)

Taylor, Elizabeth and Thomas Johnson, both of Harford County, married 17
Nov 1796 (they were married by virtue of a license issued on 12 Nov 1796)

Taylor, Hannah and Daniel McComas (son of Alexander) married 15 Mar 1753
(his name was listed in the parish register as Daniel Maccomas, son
Elexander)

Taylor, James, see "Louranna Taylor," q.v.

Taylor, Jean (widow) and Benjamin Legoe married 11 Dec 1723 (their marriage was listed as 4 Nov or 11 Dec 1723 in *Maryland Marriages, 1634-1777*; the earlier date could have been their intention of marriage or publication of banns)

Taylor, Keziah and Joshua Hardesty married 5 Oct 1746 (another entry in the parish register indicated Joshua Hargisty and Kezie Taylor married 6 Oct 1746)

Taylor, Louranna and Francis Shoudy married 13 Sep 1754 (their names were listed as Francis Showdy and Louzanna Taylor in my 1987 book and *Maryland Marriages, 1634-1777*; she may have been Lurene Taylor, born 1733, daughter of James Taylor)

Taylor, Mary and Dunham Cowan married 21 -- 1768 (probably married 21 Sep 1768, but the information was incomplete in the parish register)

Taylor, Moses and Nancy Durham or Durban, both of Harford County, married 27 Dec 1792 (no marriage license was found in Baltimore or Harford County to verify the spelling of her name because they were married by virtue of the publication of banns)

Taylor, Richard and Clemency Thomson, both of Harford County, married 2 Feb 1789 (her name was listed as Thompson in my 1987 book)

Taylor, Robert, son of Abraham and Dinah, born 13 Oct 1709 (although his date of birth was listed as 13 Oct 17-- in my 1987 book, it was noted as 13 Oct 1709 in *Baltimore County Families, 1659-1759*)

Taylor, Sarah and Robert Robertson married 9 Nov 1721 (his name was listed as Roberson in my 1987 book)

Tayman, Sabret and Jemima Hitchcock married 16 Jan 1742/3 (his name was misspelled Tayrman in my 1987 book)

Tayman, Sarah and Moses Byfoot married 5 Sep 1749 (her name was listed as Tayman or Layman in my 1987 book; another entry in the parish register indicated they married 27 Aug 1749; the earlier date could have been their intention of marriage or publication of banns)

Tayman, William Cammell and Ann Williams married 25 Dec 1750 (another entry in the parish register indicated William Camel Tayman and Anne Williams married in 1750, but the exact date was not given)

Teate, Brigitt and John Cope married 5 Feb 1753 (another entry in the parish register indicated marriage subsequent to November, 1752, but the exact date was not given; her name was listed as Bridget Tafe or Tate in *Maryland Marriages, 1634-1777* and in my 1987 book)

Tharp, Ann and John Griffin married 4 Mar 1753 (her name was listed as Harp in my 1987 book)

Thayer, George, see "George Thyler," q.v.

Thomas, Johannah and Rd. Sister Poess(?) married 4 Sep 1763 (his most unsual name was written in the parish register as either Rd. Sister Poess or Rd. Lister Poess and it remains an identification problem)

Thomas, Mary (Martha?) and Francis Kitely married 12 May 1751 (another entry in the parish register listed her name as Martha Thomas and indicated they married in 1751, but the exact date was not given)

Thompson, Aquilla and Catherine Whitaker married 20 Feb 1753 (her name was listed as Cathrine Whiteaker in the parish register)

Thompson, John and Anne Petty married 7 Jul 1748 (another entry in the parish register indicated they married in July 1748, but the exact date was not given)

Thomson, Clemency and Richard Taylor, both of Harford County, married 2 Feb 1789 (her name was listed as Thompson in my 1987 book)

Thornbury, Ann(e) and William Yeats married 8 Sep 1744 (another entry in the parish register indicated they married 5 Aug 1744; the earlier date could have been their intention of marriage or publication of banns)

Thornhill, Samuel and Mary Clyburn or Clybourn married 4 Feb 1747 (the date should actually be written 4 Feb 1747/8; another entry in the parish register indicated they married subsequent to 31 Jan 1748, but the exact date was not given)

Thornton, Eleanor (Mrs.) and Corbin S. Lee married 31 Jan 1754 (his name in my 1987 book did not include his middle initial)

Thrap, Mary (of Harford County) and Samuel Hickerson (of Baltimore County) married 13 Nov 1788 (her name was mistakenly listed as Throp in my 1987 book)

Thrift, John and Sarah Dorney married "in the year 1732" (this marriage was entered in the parish register among the 1752 marriages)

Thrift, Mary, see "William Thrift" and "Sarah Thrift," q.v.

Thrift, Richard, see "William Thrift" and "Sarah Thrift," q.v.

Thrift, Sarah, daughter of Richard and Mary, born 20 Oct 1717 (although her date of birth was listed as 20 Oct 17-- in my 1987 book, it was noted as 20 Oct 1717 in *Baltimore County Families, 1659-1759*)

Thrift, William, son of Richard and Mary, born 14 Jun 1714 (his name was mistakenly listed as Thrist in my 1987 book)

Thyler (Thayer?), George and Cathrine Graves married 1 Jan 1748 (the date should actually be written 1 Jan 1748/9; another entry in the parish register indicated George Thayer and Katherine Graves married some time between November and December, 1748, but the exact date was not given; the earlier date could have been their intention of marriage or publication of banns)

Tilley, Elizabeth, see "Joseph Greenway," q.v.

Tipper (Tapper?), Mary and George Palmer married 30 Aug 1761 (her name was difficult to read in the parish register and it could have been Tipper or Tapper)

Tolley, James Walter and Susanna Howard married 21 May 1799 (they were married by virtue of a license issued on 18 May 1799)

Tolley, Martha Susanna and Thomas Gassaway Howard, both of Baltimore County, married 2 Apr 1793 (they were married by virtue of a license issued on 1 Apr 1793 and listed her name as Martha Tolly; it should also be noted that *Baltimore County Marriage Licenses, 1777-1798* mistakenly listed her name was Tally)

Tomley (Tomlin?), Elizabeth and James Steel married 3 Feb 1743 (the date should actually be written 3 Feb 1743/4; another entry in the parish register indicated they married 29 Jan 1744 and her name was listed as Tomlin; her name was listed as Tornley or Tomley in my 1987 book)

Toomy, John and Sarah Gouldsmith married 10 Nov 1768 (another entry in the parish register listed her name was Salley)

Towson, Rachel and Thomas Bayley, Jr. married 26 Dec 1758 (his name was mistakenly listed as Thomas Bayley Bayley, Jr. in the parish register and in my 1987 book)

Tracy, Benjamin and Temperance Edwards married 13 May 1770 (their names were actually listed as Benn Trasy and Tempy Edwards in the parish register)

Trapnell, Vincent and Martha Bosley married 20 Nov 1768 (her name was mistakenly listed as Marth Bozley in my 1987 book)

Trevis (Travis), John and Ann Kelsey married 6 Dec 1743 (another entry in the parish register indicated John Travis and Anne Kelsey married 27 Nov 1743; the earlier date could have been their intention of marriage or publication of banns)

Tridge, Mary and Coleworth Kenhan married 7 Jul 1744 (his name was listed as Kenhan or Kerrhan in my 1987 book)

Tucker, Seaborn and Elizabeth Hitchcock married 9 Nov 1762 (his name was mistakenly listed as Tuckin in my 1987 book)

Tucker, Susannah and Mordicai Crawford married 16 Sep 1750 (her name was mistakenly listed as Suhannah in my 1987 book)

Tucker, William and Clement Beck married 9 Feb 1762 (her name was recorded as Clement Beck in the parish register, but this could have been Clemency Beck, born 1742, daughter of Matthew Beck)

Tudor, Dorcas and Abraham Wright married 23 May 1745 (her name was misspelled Toder in my 1987 book; another entry in the parish register spelled her name Darkes Tuder and indicated they married 14 Apr 1745; the earlier date could have been their intention of marriage or publication of banns)

Tudor, Joshua and Susanna McCubbins, both of Baltimore County, married 9 Oct 1792 (they were married by virtue of a "licence from Balto. County dated instant" as noted in the parish register; the marriage license was issued on 6 Oct 1792 and listed her name as Susannah)

Tudor, Polley and John McCubbin, both of Baltimore County, married 27 Dec 1791 (her name was listed as Tuder in one part of the parish register; they were married by virtue of a license issued on 24 Dec 1791 which listed her name as Tudor)

Tunis, Phebe and Patrick Whealand, Patrick married 6 Aug 1767 (his name was listed as Pat. in the parish register and her last name was partially blemished and could have been Tunis or perhaps Tunise or Tunish?)

Turk, Cassandra, daughter of Esau and Catharine, born 1 Mar 1784 (her father's name was mistakenly listed as Esan in my 1987 book)

Turk, John, son of Esau and Catharine, born 11 Jan 1779 (his father's name was mistakenly listed as Esan in my 1987 book)

Turner, Anne and John Beven married 6 Sep 1743 (another entry indicated they married 17 Jul 1743 and his name was listed as Bevan; the earlier date could have been their intention of marriage or publication of banns)

Turnpaw, Mary, daughter of John and Hannah, born 28 Oct 1788 (her name was mistakenly listed as Turnpace in my 1987 book)

Twine, Ann and Samuel Greening married 1 Mar 1714 (his name was listed as Grinin in my 1987 book)

Tydings, Richard and Susanna Chamberlain, both of Baltimore County, married 8 Aug 1797 (however, *Baltimore County Marriage Licenses, 1777-1798* indicated a license was issued to Richard Tydings and Susannah Hatton on 7 Aug 1797)

Underwood, Thomas and Ann(e) Petty married 31 Jul 1743 (another entry in the parish register indicated they married 1 Aug 1743)

Vance, Samuel and Mary Watters, both of Harford County, married 9 Oct 1798 (her name was mistakenly listed as Walters in my 1987 book; they were married by virtue of a license issued on 8 Oct 1798)

Vanhorn, Benjamin and Charity Sanders, both of Harford County, married 15 Feb 1791 (they were married by virtue of the publication of banns)

Vaughan, Gist and Rachael Norris married 2 Mar 1769 (his name was misspelled Vaugham in my 1987 book)

Vaunce, Andrew and Sarah Low married 4 Jan 1745 (his name was listed as Vannce in my 1987 book)

Vine, Mary and James Graham married 25 Dec 1753 (another entry in the parish register indicated they married subsequent to November, 1753, but the exact date was not given)

Vitean (Viteau?), Ann and Thomas Holland married 12 Dec 1766 (her name in the parish register could have been Vitean or Viteau)

Waddham, Elizabeth and John Almeny married 6 Feb 1753 (another entry in the parish register indicated John Almaney and Eliza Warhorn (probably misspelled) married in 1753, but the exact date was not given)

Wagstar, Mary and Thomas Niel married -- Apr 1748 (the exact date of marriage was not given, but the entry in the parish register indicated they married subsequent to 3 Apr 1748; *Maryland Marriages, 1634-1777* listed the marriage as "Thomas Niel and Mary Wagstar, April 1747, banns. pub. three times")

Waits, Frances, see "Frances White," q.v.

Waits, William Wilkinson and Susanna Stansbury, both of Baltimore County, married 4 Dec 1792 (they were married by virtue of a license issued on 7 Nov 1792 and listed his name as Waits and spelled her name Susannah; *Baltimore County Marriage Licenses, 1777-1798* mistakenly listed his name was Wails)

Waller, Elizabeth and Henry Carey married -- Jul 1746 (another entry in the parish register indicated Henry Kersey and Elizabeth Whealand married 21 Jul 1746; his name may have been Casey or Kersey although he was listed as Carey in my 1987 book; *Maryland Marriages, 1634-1777* has the marriage listed as "Henry Carey and Eliza Waller, 1746")

Wallis, Elizabeth, see "Jane Wallix (Wallis)," q.v.

Wallis, Hannah and William Brian married 5 May 1746 (another entry in the parish register indicated William Bryan and Hannah Wallace married 13 Apr 1746; the earlier date could have been their intention of marriage or publication of banns)

Wallis, Hannah and John, see "Jane Wallix (Wallis)," q.v.

Wallix (Wallis), Jane, daughter of John and Elizabeth, born 28 Nov 1741 (her name was listed as Wallix in the parish register and in my 1987 book, but in *Baltimore County Families, 1649-1759* her name was listed as Jane Wallis, born 28 Nov 1742, daughter of John and Elizabeth Wallis or Wallice (as was her sister Hannah Wallis, born 31 Jul 1744); John Wallox and Elizabeth ---- married 5 Aug 1731 and after she died in 1740 John Wallox married Elizabeth Yates on 16 Dec 1741, but she died by 4 Sep 1742 before Hannah was born; it is also possible that these were two different families that shared similar names)

Waltham, Elizabeth, see "Philizanna Waltham," q.v.

Waltham, Philizanna, daughter of Thomas and Elizabeth, born 21 Aug 1771 (her name was misspelled as Philicecanah in my 1987 book)

Waltham, Sarah and Samuel Groome Osborn married 4 Jan 1784 (this marriage was entered in the parish register among the 1754 marriages)

Waltham, Thomas and Martha Greenfield, both of Harford County, married 21 May 1795 (they were married by virtue of a license issued in Harford County on that same day; it listed her name was Patty)

Waltham, Thomas, see "Philizanna Waltham," q.v.

Walton, Joseph and Sarah Matheny married 28 Apr 1746 (another entry in the parish register indicated they married 23 Mar 1746 and listed her name as Metheny; the earlier date could have been their intention of marriage or publication of banns)

Wane, John, age 50, resident of Joppa, buried 16 Dec 1792 (his name was listed as John Wana in my 1987 book)

Ward, Elizabeth and Sollomon Whealand married 22 Feb 1766 (his name was listed as Soll. and her name as Eliz. in the parish register)

Ward, Elizabeth and William Curle married in 1775 (the exact date of marriage was not given, but their request to publish marriage banns was dated 10 Aug 1775 in the parish register)

Ward, Isaac and Anne Fields married in 1753 (the complete date was not given in the parish register)

Ward, John and Sarah Burrough married 17 Dec 1737 (her name was listed as Borrough in my 1987 book)

Ward, Joseph and Mary Perkinson married 13 Feb 1748 (the date should actually be 13 Feb 1748/9; another entry in the parish register indicated they married subsequent to 3 Feb 1749, but the exact date was not given, and her name was listed as Parkinson)

Ward, Joseph and Hannah Lee married 24 Aug 1743 (another entry in the parish register indicated they married 7 Aug 1743 and his name was listed as Jr.;

the earlier date could have been their intention of marriage or publication of banns)

Ward, Mary and Richard Menson married 24 Mar 1763 (his name was listed in the parish register as either Rd. Menson or Rd. Minson)

Wareing, Ann(e) and James Skipper married 10 Nov 1753 (another entry in the parish register indicated James Skipen and Anne Warring married in 1753, but the exact date was not given)

Warhorn, Eliza, see "Elizabeth Waddham," q.v.

Warren, John and Elizabeth Keen or Cane married 16 Feb 1751 (another entry in the parish register indicated they married in 1751, but the exact date was not given)

Warring, Anne, see "Ann Wareing," q.v.

Waters, Elizabeth and Thomas Birkhead, both of Baltimore County, married 7 Dec 1797 (they were married by virtue of a license issued on 4 Dec 1797; *Baltimore County Marriage Licenses, 1777-1798* mistakenly listed his name as Bukhead)

Waters, Henry and Grace Wilson, both of Harford County, married 21 Feb 1792 (they were married by virtue of a license issued on that same day)

Waters, Martha and John Rockhold, both of Harford County, married 2 Feb 1790 (his name looked like Borkhold in one part of the parish register, but it was Rockhold as listed in *Maryland Marriages, 1778-1800*)

Watkins, Daniel and Sosia Biddeston married 3 May 1770 (his name was listed as Danial in my 1987 book and her name was actually Presioca Biddison, daughter of Thomas Biddison)

Watkins, Jane and Jos. White married 7 Aug 1766 (his name was unclear in the parish register, but listed as Jos. in *Maryland Marriages, 1634-1777* and mistakenly listed as Jas. in my 1987 book)

Watkins, John and Ruth Guyton, both of Baltimore County, married 2 Jun 1796 (they were married by virtue of a license issued on 31 May 1796)

Watkins, William and Anne Blackaby married in summer of 1742 "on W. Carbel's land" (see the following William Watkins entry; the women's names sound quite similar)

Watkins, William and Ann Barkabee married 9 Dec 1741 (this marriage was entered in the parish register among the 1752 marriages; see the preceding William Watkins entry; the women's names sound quite similar)

Watson, Jane, wife of John, died 23 Dec 1732 (he had married Jean Scott in 1729 and although the date of her death was entered in the parish register as 23 Dec 1732/3 this is incorrect because "double dating" applied only to dates from 1 Jan to 24 Mar in the old style calendar)

Watson, John, see "Jane Watson," q.v.

Watson, Thomas and Frances Hooper married 24 Mar 1761 (her name was listed as Fra. in the parish register and his name was spelled Wattson in my 1987 book)

Watters, Mary and Samuel Vance, both of Harford County, married 9 Oct 1798 (her name was mistakenly listed as Walters in my 1987 book; they were married by virtue of a license issued on 8 Oct 1798)

Wear, James and Charity Key, both of Harford County, married 11 Sep 1791 (they were married by virtue of the publication of banns)

Weatherel, William and Mary Presbury, both of Harford County, married 21 Sep 1797 (his name was listed as William Witherall in my 1987 book; a marriage license was issued to William Weatherall and Mary Presbury on 19 Sep 1797)

Weeks, Daniel and Nancy Lecester married 10 Sep 1771 (his name was listed as Wheeks in the parish register and her name was listed as Lueester in my 1987 book)

Weeks, Lucretia and Thomas Nash, both of Harford County, married 25 Dec 1788 (her name was mistakenly listed as Wicks in my 1987 book)

Weeks, Sarah and James Malloy, both of Harford County, married 13 Aug 1789 (her name was mistakenly listed in my 1987 book as Wicks and their marriage date was listed as 10 Aug 1789; his name was listed as Mulloy in another part of the parish register)

Weeks, Thomas and Elizabeth Enlowe married 12 Dec 1742 (another entry in the parish register indicated Thomas Wicks and Elizabeth Enlow married 15 Dec 1742; his name was spelled Weekes in my 1987 book)

Wein (Weir?), John and Elizabeth Godard married 8 Jan 1760 (his name could have been Ween, Wein or Weir in the parish register)

Welch, Cassandra and John Carroll married 24 Dec 1760 (his name was listed as Jno. and her name was listed as Cas. in the parish register)

Welch, Laban and Leah Corbin married 3 Sep 1761 (his name could have been Welch or Welsh in the parish register)

Welcher, John and Ann Foreasjute married 24 Apr 1764 (her last name was most unusual and difficult to read in the parish register)

Wells, Elizabeth and Joseph Renshaw married 28 Oct 1742 (his name was misspelled Reneher in my 1987 book)

Wells, Joseph and Ann Carback married 30 Jan 1748 (the date should actually be written 30 Jan 1748/9; another entry in the parish register indicated they married some time between December, 1748 and February, 1749, but the exact date was not given; the earlier date could have been their intention of marriage or publication of banns)

Wells, Zenas and Elizabeth Flanagan married 5 Sep 1799 (his name was mistakenly listed once as Thomas in my 1987 book and then as Zenas in another part of that book; their marriage license was issued 4 Sep 1799; *Maryland Marriages, 1634-1777* first listed her name as Hanazan and then indicated Flanagan)

West, Sybell and Francis Holland, both of Baltimore County, married 25 May 1797 (they were married by virtue of a license issued on 18 May 1797)

Wetheral, Henry and Mrs. Mary Chamberlain married 20 Dec 1722 (his name was listed as Witheral and at times as Witherall in the parish register; their marriage date was listed as 20 Dec 172- in my 1987 book)

Wharton, John and Ann Brown married 28 Jan 1744 (another entry in the parish register indicated they married 28 Jan 1745 and her name was listed as Anne; the date should actually be written 28 Jan 1744/5)

Whealand, Henry and Isabell Willson married 21 Jul 1764 (his name was listed as Hen. and her name was listed as Isbell in the parish register)

Whealand, Patrick and Mary Cowdry married 26 Jan 1749 (the date should actually be 26 Jan 1740/50; another entry in the parish register indicated they married some time between 17 Dec 1749 and 11 Feb 1750, but the exact date was not given; her name was mistakenly listed as Candry in my 1987 book)

Whealand, Patrick and Phebe Tunis married 6 Aug 1767 (his name was listed as Pat. in the parish register and her last name was partially blemished and could have been Tunis or perhaps Tunise or Tunish?)

Whealand, Sarah and Francis Flannen married 2 Oct 1748 (another entry in the parish register indicated Francis Flannel and Sarah Whaland married subsequent to 4 Sep 1748, but the exact date was not given)

Whealand, Sollomon and Elizabeth Copeland married 18 Jan 1761 (his name was listed as Sollo. and her name was listed as Eliz. in the parish register)

Whealand, Sollomon and Elizabeth Ward married 22 Feb 1766 (his name was listed as Soll. and her name as Eliz. in the parish register)

Whealand, William and Mary Legoe married 21 Apr 1752 (another entry in the parish register indicated they married subsequent to November, 1751, but the exact date was not given, and his name was listed as Whaland)

Wheeks, Daniel, see "Daniel Weeks," q.v.

Wheeler, Elizabeth and Caleb Bosley married 27 Feb 1772 (his name was listed as Calib Bozley in the parish register)

Wheeler, Rebecca and William Smith married 26 Nov 1772 (her name was listed as Whelar in the parish register)

Whicks, John and Mary Petetow married 24 Jan 1765 (his name in the parish register appeared to be either Jno. Whicks or Wheeks)

Whips, Samuel and Mary McComas married 22 Jan 1742 (their names were listed as Samuel Whipps and Mary Maccomas in my 1987 book)

Whitaker, Abraham and Ann Poteet married 15 Jul 1725 (their names were listed as Abraham Wittacre and Ann Puttee in the parish register)

Whitaker, Catherine and Aquilla Thompson married 20 Feb 1753 (her name was listed as Cathrine Whiteaker in the parish register)

Whitaker, Hannah, see "Alexander McComas," q.v.

Whitaker, John, died 30 Nov 1713 (his name was listed as Whittacar in my 1987 book)

Whitaker, John, see "Joshua Johnson Whitaker," q.v.

Whitaker, Joshua Johnson, son of John and Rachel, born 5 Aug 1790 (the year was listed as 1791 in my 1987 book, but it could have been 1790; John Whitacre and Rachel Johnson were married by virtue of a license issued in Harford County on 6 Sep 1780)

Whitaker, Mary and Daniel Butler married 4 Oct 1747 (another entry in the parish register indicated they married 23 Aug 1747; the earlier date could have been their intention of marriage or publication of banns)

Whitaker, Peter and Emelie Hitchcock married 12 Feb 1744 (another entry in the parish register indicated they married 10 Feb 1745 and her name was listed as Amelia; the date should actually be written 12 Feb 1744/5)

Whitaker, Rachel, see "Joshua Johnson Whitaker," q.v.

Whitaker, Sarah and Benjamin Norris married 8 Oct 1719 (her last name was not indicated in the parish register and in my 1987 book, but *Baltimore County Families, 1659-1759* indicated her name was Whitaker)

White, Frances and John Demmitt married 5 Aug 1759 (her name was difficult to read in the parish register and it could have been White or Waits)

White, Comfort and John Brown married 21 Feb 1747 (the date should actually be written 21 Feb 1747/8; another entry in the parish register indicated they married subsequent to 31 Jan 1748, but the exact date was not given)

White, Delilah and William Godwin, both of Harford County, married 22 Jul 1797 (although the parish register indicated their names were William Godman and Deliah White, *Harford County Marriage Licenses, 1777-1865* indicated a license was issued to Wm. Godwin and Delilah White on 15 Jul 1797)

White, Dinah and Abraham Taylor married 20 -- 1708? (their date of marriage was incomplete in the parish register and even though it was listed among the marriages and births circa 1713-1714, their first child Robert was born 13 Oct 1709, as noted in *Baltimore County Families, 1659-1759*)

White, John and Mary Horton married in 1749 (the exact date was not given in the parish register, but apparently they married some time between 26 Mar and 14 May 1749)

White, John and Sarah Legoe married 4 Oct 1744 (another entry in the parish register indicated they married 23 Sep 1744; the earlier date could have been their intention of marriage or publication of banns)

White, John and Elizabeth or Betty Gott married 29 Jan 1751 (another entry in the parish register indicated they married in 1751, but the exact date was not given)

White, John Jr. and Ann Yeates married 12 May 1751 (this marriage was inadvertently omitted from my 1987 book)

White, Jos. and Jane Watkins married 7 Aug 1766 (his name was unclear in the parish register, but listed as Jos. in *Maryland Marriages, 1634-1777* and mistakenly listed as Jas. in my 1987 book)

White, Stephen and Hannah Baker married 1 Jan 1751 (another entry in the parish register indicated they married in 1751, but the exact date was not given)

Whiteford, Robert and Nancy McCairman, both of Harford County, married 2 Feb 1796 (they were mistakenly listed as Robert Whitfoed and ---- McCarman in my 1987 book; they were married by virtue of a license issued that same day and it listed her name as Kerman)

Whitehead, William Bond and Susannah Wood married 26 Feb 1749 (another entry in the parish register indicated they married subsequent to 17 Dec 1749, but the exact date was not given; her name was mistakenly listed as Suhannah in my 1987 book)

Wiat, Richard and Dinah Corbin married 10 May 1772 (his name was mistakenly listed as Wist in my 1987 book)

Wicks, Sarah, see "Sarah Weeks," q.v.

Wicks, Thomas, see "Thomas Weeks," q.v.

Wiley, John, see "John Wyle," q.v.

Wilkinson, Jethro Lynch and Elizabeth Merryman married 29 Jan 1761 (her name was listed as Eliz. Marryman in the parish register)

Wilkinson, Samuel and Mary Asher married 14 Apr 1748 (another entry in the parish register indicated they married 3 Jan 1748; the earlier date could have been their intention of marriage or publication of banns)

Williams, Ann(e) and William Cammell Tayman married 25 Dec 1750 (another entry in the parish register indicated William Camel Tayman and Anne Williams married in 1750, but the exact date was not given)

Williams, John and Ruth Rockhold married 17 Apr 1749 (another entry in the parish register indicated they married some time between 26 Mar and 14 May 1749, but the exact date was not given)

Williams, Mary and William Henderside married 18 Aug 1771 (their request to publish marriage banns was entered in the parish register on 27 Jul 1771 and his name was subsequently listed as Handerside)

Williams, Richard and Ann(e) Nairne married 12 Jun 1746 (another entry in the parish register gave the same information, but listed her name as Ann Nearn)

Williams, Sarah and John Jeffreys married 14 Nov 1749 (his name was misspelled Jeffriys in my 1987 book; another entry in the parish register indicated they married 28 May 1749 and his name was listed as Jeffrey; the earlier date could have been their intention of marriage or publication of banns)

Williams, William and Sarah Ellwood married 8 Dec 1748 (another entry in the parish register indicated they married in December 1748, but the day was not given)

Williams, William and Mary Rynoo married 6 -- 1768 (probably married 6 Oct 1768, but the information was incomplete in the parish register)

Willion, John and Rachael Rigbie or Rigbee married 10 Nov 1763 (his name was difficult to read in the parish register and it could have been Jno. Willion or Jno. Willson)

Willson, Isabell and Henry Whealand married 21 Jul 1764 (his name was listed as Hen. and her name was listed as Isbell in the parish register)

Wilmer, Benjamin and Margaret Crawford married 29 May 1800 (they were married by virtue of a license issued on 28 May 1800)

Wilson, Grace and Henry Waters, both of Harford County, married 21 Feb 1792 (they were married by virtue of a license issued on that same day)

Wilson, Henry and Sarah Worthington, both of Baltimore County, married 9 Apr 1795 (they were married by virtue of a license issued in Baltimore County on 4 Apr 1795)

Wilson (Willson), Sarah and John Swinard married 30 Apr 1747 (his name was mistakenly listed as Surnard in my 1987 book; another entry in the parish register indicated they married 12 Apr 1747; the earlier date could have been their intention of marriage or publication of banns)

Wittacre, Abraham, see "Abraham Whitaker," q.v.

Wittacre, Hannah, see "Hannah Whitaker," q.v.

Woaler, John and Frances Brannan married 4 Apr 1768 (his name was listed as Woaler in my 1987 book and as Wooler in *Maryland Marriages, 1634-1777*, but it looked liked Waaler in the parish register)

Wodgworth, Thomas and Rebecca Pasmore married -- Jan 1741 (his name was listed as Wordgworth in other parts of the parish register)

Wood, Ann and John Cotterrel married 14 Jun 1752 (another entry in the parish register indicated John Cotrall and Anne Wood married subsequent to May 1752, but the exact date was not given)

Wood, Henry and Susannah Ramsey married 3 Nov 1766 (her last name was not listed in the parish register when they were married, but it was listed when their request to publish marriage banns was entered in the parish register on 20 Jul 1766)

Wood, Rebecca and James Brown married 31 May 1767 (her name was listed as Reba. with an elevated "a" in the parish register)

Wood, Susannah and William Bond Whitehead married 26 Feb 1749 (another entry in the parish register indicated they married subsequent to 17 Dec 1749, but the exact date was not given; her name was mistakenly listed as Suhannah in my 1987 book)

Woodard, Ann and Thomas Presbury married -- Dec 1749 (this marriage was entered in the parish register among the December, 1750 marriages)

Woodland, James and Sarah Collins, both of Harford County, married 25 Dec 1792 (they were married by virtue of the publication of banns)

Woodland, Joseph and Cassandra Massey married 7 Jul 1772 (her name was listed as Masscey in the parish register)

Woodland, Martha and John Dorsey married 18 Dec 1770 (their names were listed as John Dorcey and Marth Woodland in my 1987 book)

Woolling, Amelia and Thomas O'Brian married 14 Jun 1757 (his name was listed as Thos. Obrian in the parish register)

Worrell, Thomas and Mary Conden, both of Baltimore County, married 12 May 1788 (his name was listed as Worrall in my 1987 book)

Worthington, Ann and Weymouth Shaw married 23 Apr 1761 (his name was listed as Weymoth in the parish register)

Worthington, Sarah and Henry Wilson, both of Baltimore County, married 9 Apr 1795 (they were married by virtue of a license issued in Baltimore County on 4 Apr 1795)

Wright, Abraham and Darkes or Dorcas Tuder married 23 May 1745 (her name was misspelled Toder in my 1987 book; another entry in the parish register indicated they married 14 Apr 1745; the earlier date could have been their intention of marriage or publication of banns)

Wright, Elizabeth and Heathcot Pickett married 26 Jan 1742 (his name was misspelled Heathcut in my 1987 book and their names were listed as Heathcote Pickett and Eliz. Wright in *Maryland Marriages, 1634-1777*)

Wright, Elizabeth and John Elliott married 22 Dec 1761 (the date of marriage was mistakenly listed as 23 Dec in my 1987 book)

Wright, John and Rebecca Othasson or Otherson, both of Harford County, married 21 Aug 1791 (although her name was listed as Othasson in one part of the parish register, a marriage license issued in Baltimore County on 17 Aug 1791 listed her name as Otherson)

Wright, Joseph and Margaret James married in 1750 (the complete date was not given in the parish register)

Wright, Manerlin and John Copass married 24 Jan 1742 (the date should actually be written 24 Jan 1742/3; her name was mistakenly listed as Manuell in my 1987 book; another entry in the parish register listed his name as Copas and indicated they married 16 Jan 1742; the earlier date could have been their intention of marriage or publication of banns)

Wright, Nathaniel and Sophia Rutledge married 11 Apr 1769 (her name was listed as Rutlege in the parish register)

Wright, Rachel and William Carvin married 15 Aug 1745 (another entry in the parish register indicated William Corbin and Rachel Wright married 11 Aug 1745)

Wright, Sarah and John Jarvis married 2 Jul 1761 (his name was listed as Jno. Jarves in the parish register)

Wright, Thomas and Ann Green, both of Harford County, married 17 Mar 1791 (they were married by virtue of a license issued in Harford County on 16 Mar 1791)

Wright, William and Juliana Benbow married 5 Sep 1714 (their names were listed as William Right and Juliana Benbo in my 1987 book)

Wright, William, see "Philip Lock Elliott," q.v.

Wyle, Auther and John Stevenson married 11 Aug 1763 (her name was entered as Auther or Anther in the parish register and in my 1987 book; she could have been Athea Wyle, daughter of Luke Wyle)

Wyle, John and Elizabeth Perdue married 12 May 1748 (another entry in the parish register indicated John Wiley and Elizabeth Perdue married 3 Apr 1748; the earlier date could have been their intention of marriage or publication of banns)

Wyle, Luke, see "Auther Wyle," q.v.

Wyle, Walter and Susannah Norris married 29 Dec 1763 (his name was written as Walt. Wyle in the parish register)

Yarley, Ralph and Ruth Burton, both of Baltimore County, married 24 Dec 1795 (her name was mistakenly listed as Barton in my 1987 book; they were married by virtue of a license issued on 19 Dec 1795 which listed his name as Yarly)

Yarley, Rebecca and John Lawrence, both of Baltimore County, married 5 Jul 1795 (they were married by virtue of the publication of banns)

Yates, Elizabeth, see "Jane Wallix (Wallis)," q.v.

Yates, William, see "William Yeates," q.v.

Yeates Ann and John White, Jr. married 12 May 1751 (this marriage was inadvertently omitted from my 1987 book)

Yeates, William and Ann Dorney married 28 Apr 1748 (another entry in the parish register indicated William Yates and Anne Dorney married 24 Apr 1748)

Yeats, Mary and James Dorney married 14 Dec 1743 (another entry in the parish register indicated they married 20 Nov 1743 and his name was listed as Dawney; the earlier date could have been their intention of marriage or publication of banns)

Yeats, Thomas and Elizabeth Martin married 21 Jun 1744 (another entry in the parish register indicated they married 17 Jun 1744)

Yeats, William and Ann(e) Thornbury married 8 Sep 1744 (another entry in the parish register indicated they married 5 Aug 1744; the earlier date could have been their intention of marriage or publication of banns)

York, Edward and Anne Dorney married 21 Oct 1742 (another entry in the parish register indicated they married 26 Sep 1742; the earlier date could have been their intention of marriage or publication of banns)

York, George, son of George and Susannah, born 1712 (his name was listed as Yoark in my 1987 book and his date of birth was not complete in the parish register)

York, George and Lettice Doddridge married 7 May 1721 (her name was listed as Dawdridge in my 1987 book)

York, John and Sarah Horner married 16 Oct 1752 (the year was clearly written as 1752 in the parish register, but the information was entered among the October, 1751 marriages)

York, Rebecca and Jonathan Eddee married 4 Apr 1743 (his name was listed as Edy and Ady in other parts of the parish register and another entry in the parish register indicated Jonathan Ady and Rebeccah York married 27 Mar 1743; the earlier date could have been their intention of marriage or publication of banns)

York, Sarah and John Day (son of Edward) married 30 Dec 1764 (another entry in the parish register indicated they were married about 4 o'clock in the afternoon)

York, Susannah, see "George York," q.v.

Young, Clara and Paul Aimé Fleury, both of Baltimore County, married 28 Oct 1794 (his name was listed as Paul Aimee Fleury and her name as Clare Young in another part of the parish register; marriage license was issued to Mr. Fleury and Clara Young on 11 Oct 1794)

Young, Rebecca and Nicholas Cleggett married 11 Feb 1768 (his name was listed as Nichs. and her name was listed as Reba. in the parish register)

----, Catherine and Robert Shafford married 17 -- 1768 (probably married 17 Sep 1768, but the information was incomplete in the parish register)

----, Sarah and John Bevins, Jr. married -- Dec 1723 (information was incomplete in the parish register; this marriage was inadvertently omitted from *Maryland Marriages, 1634-1777*)

---- and Samuel Stevens married Shrove Tuesday, 1723 (information was incomplete in the parish register; this marriage was inadvertently omitted from *Maryland Marriages, 1634-1777*)

---- and William Smith married 17 -- 1768 (information was incomplete in the parish register; probably married 17 Sep 1768)

Marylanders to Kentucky, 1775-1825

Methodist Records of Baltimore City, Maryland: Volume 1, 1799-1829

Methodist Records of Baltimore City, Maryland: Volume 2, 1830-1839

*Methodist Records of Baltimore City, Maryland: Volume 3, 1840-1850
(East City Station)*

More Maryland Deponents, 1716-1799

*More Marylanders to Carolina: Migration of Marylanders to
North Carolina and South Carolina prior to 1800*

More Marylanders to Kentucky, 1778-1828

Outpensioners of Harford County, Maryland, 1856-1896

Presbyterian Records of Baltimore City, Maryland, 1765-1840

Quaker Records of Baltimore and Harford Counties, Maryland, 1801-1825

Quaker Records of Northern Maryland, 1716-1800

Quaker Records of Southern Maryland, 1658-1800

Revolutionary Patriots of Anne Arundel County, Maryland

Revolutionary Patriots of Baltimore Town and Baltimore County, 1775-1783

Revolutionary Patriots of Calvert and St. Mary's Counties, Maryland, 1775-1783

Revolutionary Patriots of Caroline County, Maryland, 1775-1783

Revolutionary Patriots of Cecil County, Maryland

Revolutionary Patriots of Charles County, Maryland, 1775-1783

Revolutionary Patriots of Delaware, 1775-1783

Revolutionary Patriots of Dorchester County, Maryland, 1775-1783

Revolutionary Patriots of Frederick County, Maryland, 1775-1783

Revolutionary Patriots of Harford County, Maryland, 1775-1783

Revolutionary Patriots of Kent and Queen Anne's Counties

Revolutionary Patriots of Lancaster County, Pennsylvania

Revolutionary Patriots of Maryland, 1775-1783: A Supplement

Revolutionary Patriots of Maryland, 1775-1783: Second Supplement

Revolutionary Patriots of Montgomery County, Maryland, 1776-1783

Revolutionary Patriots of Prince George's County, Maryland, 1775-1783

Revolutionary Patriots of Talbot County, Maryland, 1775-1783

Revolutionary Patriots of Worcester and Somerset Counties, Maryland, 1775-1783

Revolutionary Patriots of Washington County, Maryland, 1776-1783

*St. George's (Old Spesutia) Parish, Harford County, Maryland:
Church and Cemetery Records, 1820-1920*

St. John's and St. George's Parish Registers, 1696-1851

Survey Field Book of David and William Clark in Harford County, Maryland, 1770-1812

The Crenshaws of Kentucky, 1800-1995

The Delaware Militia in the War of 1812

*Union Chapel United Methodist Church Cemetery Tombstone Inscriptions,
Wilna, Harford County, Maryland*